SHE GOT GAME

MY PERSONAL ODYSSEY

CYNTHIA COOPER

WARNER BOOKS

A Time Warner Company

Grateful acknowledgment is given to Eric Cooper for permission to reprint the rap on page 178.

Warner Books, Inc., 1271 Avenue of the Americas, New York, NY 10020

Visit our Web site, Time Warner Bookmark, at www.twbookmark.com

 A Time Warner Company

Printed in the United States of America

First Printing: August 1999

10 9 8 7 6 5 4 3 2 1

Library of Congress Cataloging-in-Publication Data

Cooper, Cynthia.
    She got game : my personal odyssey / Cynthia Cooper.
      p. cm.
    Includes index.
    ISBN 0-446-52566-9
    1. Cooper, Cynthia, 1963 Apr. 14– 2. Basketball players—United States—
Biography.   3. Women basketball players—United States—Biography.   I. Title.
GV884.C63A3   1999
796.323'092—dc21
    [B]   99-18907
                                                                        CIP

Book design: H. Roberts Design

To my mother, Mary Cobbs, for teaching me I can do all things through Christ Jesus, who gives me strength. And to children everywhere who dream of making a better life for themselves.

Acknowledgments

Special thanks to Molly Sanchez of the USC sports information office, Tom Savage of the Houston Comets and Mark Pray of the WNBA. The authors also deeply appreciate the contributions of Angela Allin, Mary Cobbs, Anthony Falsone, Kim Perrot, Linda Sharp, Angela Wigington, Leland "Pookey" Wigington, Fred Williams and Rhonda Windham. And the assistance of Cynthia Cooper's nieces and nephews, especially Brenda McNeal. We are grateful to Monica Reeves, who offered invaluable advice at several critical junctures. Finally, thanks to Scott Waxman of Scott Waxman Agency, Timothy Sims of Baseline Sports and Rick Wolff of Warner Books.

Contents

Chapter One

My Time to Shine

The one thing that drives me and keeps me motivated is that I've always been the underdog. Always. Growing up in a large family of eight kids, I was the overlooked middle child. One of my four older siblings or three younger ones always seemed to be the center of attention. Never me.

I was a shy and introverted little girl, not comfortable with how I looked or what I had to say. I felt insignificant. I tried to hide my pain by keeping to myself and masking my feelings.

I was an underdog in basketball, too. Playing in college, on U.S. national teams and for more than a decade in the European professional leagues, I took a back seat to others. Even when I became a leading scorer in Europe and one of the top players overseas, I never received much publicity or notice. There were always bigger names around, drawing most of the attention.

My time to shine wasn't in college or on the national teams. I had to play a supporting role to help those teams become successful. I never was the go-to player or what fans and media would consider the star.

But now, playing in the WNBA, my time to shine has finally arrived. I've become the kind of player I always wanted to be and dreamed I could be. During the many long years I spent out of the spotlight, watching other players receive all the honors and recognition, I kept telling myself, "I am not less of a player or less of a person. I am going to continue to work on my game, I am going to grow as a person and I'm going to show everyone who I really am and—wait a minute, hold on—I've got a little bit of personality, too."

I am no longer that timid and shy little girl who grew up in the inner city of Los Angeles, unsure of herself, unsure of her future, not knowing where she was going and without direction or purpose.

That little girl, a true underdog, has become a distant memory.

I know what I want. I want to play to the best of my ability and be a leader for my Houston teammates. I want to promote women's basketball and help market the WNBA. I want to provide a better future for my family, especially my nieces and nephews who live with my mother and me in the suburbs of Houston.

I also want to serve as a role model for kids in the inner city who think their lives are hopeless or there's no way out.

If I don't know anything else—and there are a lot of things I don't know—I know where I'm going in life. I am going to succeed and excel. And I would love to bring along with me every single person who is scared or unsure or uncertain of themselves.

If someone feels surrounded by life or trapped in a bad situation, or if they think they can't possibly succeed, I am here to tell that person she or he can escape from that bad situation.

Each of us has within ourselves the power to make a better, brighter life.

I know, because I did it.

People never had great expectations for me. Most of the people I knew growing up would give me a million reasons why I shouldn't succeed instead of giving me one reason why I should.

But despite the negativity that surrounded my life in the inner city—the gangs, drugs and violence—I believed in myself. I established goals as a basketball player and a person. I didn't want to prove my doubters wrong as much as I wanted to prove that I was right.

I've noticed that a lot of people get sidetracked worrying about what others say about them. They get hung up worrying about people's opinions of what they can or can't accomplish. They get discouraged by listening to people talk about their supposed shortcomings and limitations.

I learned long ago that I can't control what other people think or say. But I can control what I think and say, and what I do in my life. I can control where I'm headed.

Rather than listening to others, people need to learn to focus on what they can do, what they want to do and how they can go about accomplishing whatever it is they want to accomplish.

That's where I keep my focus: what I want to do and how I'm going to do it.

The success of the Houston Comets and the WNBA has given me the opportunity to make a difference and to have an impact on the lives of our youth. Not only with my nieces and nephews but on the lives of youth in America and internationally. My success in women's basketball has given me the chance to leave my mark on the world in a positive light.

It's also given me a chance, for the first time in my life, to be me. I can say what I mean and mean what I say. It's the real me that has come out since the Houston Comets emerged as back-to-back WNBA champions.

It's not the middle child. It's not the role player. It's not the basketball player overshadowed by her teammates. It's not an underdog—it's the real me. I have taken on responsibility as a WNBA leader, as a daughter and an aunt. I'm making the decisions for my own life. I'm the one who's accountable.

I know what I want to accomplish and where I want to go. When I don't know the answers to the questions I face, I'm not afraid to ask for help. I no longer feel, as I once did, that asking questions makes you less of a person or that it means you're dumb, ignorant or stupid.

I've discovered that it's the person who doesn't ask questions who is ignorant, because he or she remains that way.

Two years ago, before the Houston Comets became one of the hottest teams in professional sports, I was just an average, everyday person. I could go anywhere and do anything without being recognized or stopped on the street. I didn't have to worry about marketing people, marketing agreements and contracts. I didn't have to worry about book deals and movie deals. I didn't have to worry about the correct wording in a contract. But I've had to learn all that.

The only way to learn is to not be scared about speaking up when you don't understand something. To ask questions and to not be fooled by someone telling you it's not your responsibility, that an agent or a marketing company will handle things.

It *is* your responsibility. Everything we do is our own responsibility.

What I learned from the example my mother, Mary Cobbs, set for me—besides how to work hard, make sacrifices, trust in the Lord and take responsibility for my actions—is that each of us can do more.

Doing more is one message I take to audiences whenever

I'm invited to spea̶̶̶̶̶̶̶̶̶̶ to have to beg people to let me speak at their scho̶̶̶̶̶̶̶̶̶̶̶̶̶̶ fund-raising events. Now, after the success of the Houston Comets and the individual recognition I've received, people are begging me to talk.

"You can achieve something more," I say. "You can always get better. You can be a better friend to your friends, a better sister to your brothers, a better daughter to your parents. When you realize you can do more tomorrow than you're doing today, you will get inspired. You'll develop a fire within yourself, a desire to become a better person, a better doctor, lawyer or athlete. You'll have a hunger and thirst for knowledge. Because knowledge is power."

I've had people come up to me after my speeches and tell me they've been inspired. A woman who recently heard me speak at a church in Houston told me afterward that I'd motivated her to go back to college and finish her degree. It's gratifying to think that I'm having a positive impact on some people's lives, that I'm able to make a difference.

There's one other message I try to stress in speeches: Don't put limits on yourself. Reach as high as you can. Keep raising the bar.

After spending more than a decade in Europe, I had every reason to come back to the United States and not play at such a high level. I was thirty-four years old when the WNBA started in 1997, an age at which many women basketball players have already turned to coaching or other pursuits.

Many people associated with women's basketball thought my best years were behind me. It would have been easy for me to go along with that line of thinking and say, "Hey, you know what? They're right. I'm not in my prime anymore."

I wouldn't do it. I wouldn't accept that thinking. I've spent a lot of years paying my dues in women's basketball; when the WNBA got under way, it was time to collect.

The number one thing I wanted to do in the WNBA was

show everyone I could play basketball at the high level I'd maintained in Europe. I wanted my family and friends, especially my mother, to see how my game has grown and matured since I was the sparkplug sixth man on the USC Lady Trojans NCAA championship teams in the early 1980s.

The past two years have been like a dream fulfilled. Words could never express how it feels to play in front of a sold-out Houston crowd of 16,285 people who worship every move you make and every shot you take. Fans who give you unconditional support.

Words can't explain how it feels to have people chanting in unison, "MVP! MVP! MVP!" Hearing that brought tears to my eyes at the free throw line. It was like a wake-up call to what was happening, because I get so wrapped up in the game I don't realize the magnitude of it all. It's truly awesome.

To see where we've come from and where women's basketball is going and the immense opportunity we now have brings joy to my heart. And some sadness, too, because there are a lot of great women players this opportunity has passed by.

Just to be part of the WNBA is special, but to actually excel and go down in history as the league's first superstar is amazing. It's special to me and my family, and it's even more gratifying because my mother has been part of it.

As many basketball fans already know, Mary Cobbs was diagnosed with breast cancer shortly before the WNBA began its inaugural season. It's been a difficult period for our family, but the success of the Comets and the accolades for her daughter have brought joy to Mother's life and helped her fight in the battle with cancer.

Some WNBA players probably take what the league has going for granted, but I'm not one of them. I've been through the wringer playing basketball. I've had to survive a lot of tough times—like being forced to go abroad to pursue my dream and having to stay overseas so long, in a different culture, away from family and friends.

Circumstances forced me to lose touch with people I grew up with. Those are years and experiences I can never replace.

Since I made all those sacrifices, I'm able to appreciate the WNBA and the opportunities that we have more than most. It's my job now to make sure the next generation of women basketball players, and the generations after it, don't have to go overseas.

That could be an option, certainly, but it would no longer be a necessity. If we handle things right, women basketball players will be able to stay home and live in America and make a living doing something they love to do.

To me, this book is about finding yourself, believing in yourself and awakening to the fact that it's you who determines your future and what you do with your life. You can take control.

I got off to a slow start. I was a true underdog, unsteady and unsure of myself. Once I gained some self-confidence and learned to believe in myself, I began to soar.

I know you can, too. Just follow me.

Chapter Two

Like Mother, Like Daughter

I get my drive and determination to succeed and excel directly from my mother, Mary Cobbs.

I saw my mother raise eight children to the best of her ability as a single parent. I watched her work from morning to night—at times it seemed as if she worked twenty-four hours a day—to support us.

She worked as a custodian for the Rapid Transit Department in Los Angeles. She cleaned homes and did odd jobs on the side.

I saw my mother get stressed out by trying to make ends meet. She had to see to it that our bills were paid and we had food on the table and clothes on our back and shoes on our feet. And that when any of us were sick, we got to see the doctor.

My mother shouldered most of the burdens in our family. And she did so for a long, long time—as long as I can remember.

Her hard work inspired me. So did her attitude. Because no matter how difficult things were, or how dark the situation, or how much she had to sacrifice, she would never give up.

She would not allow herself to fail.

I know a lot of children expect their parents to tell them some meaningful story, or say some magical word, to give them inspiration and motivation. Kids often need to hear some encouraging words to help them get over a difficult situation or through some terrible times.

My mother never had that kind of conversation with my brothers and sisters and me. She didn't need to. Her actions spoke louder than words.

I have learned through the years that when I encounter problems and challenges, I can overcome them. Because my mother, by overcoming the tough times she experienced and never giving up, showed me how.

She worked to give us a better chance in life. No sacrifice was too great to make for her children. She would come home so tired, so exhausted by her long day's work that she'd be unable to do anything but collapse.

Because she had set goals for herself and her family, however, she would get up the next day and do it all over again—without whining or complaining or feeling sorry for herself.

She would not surrender.

When I was a little girl, we lived in the projects in Los Angeles, and Mother received welfare from the government. She eventually got off welfare and began to work and make money.

Mother was constantly doing whatever she could to improve our situation. She moved us out of the projects in Los Angeles into an apartment and later into our own house. When that house burned down, she had to move us into an apartment in Watts. But she knew the environment there was violent and tough, so she saved up enough money to buy us another house.

Because of the circumstances she faced, my mother wasn't able to give her children all the love and attention and nurturing she would have wanted to. That bothered me a lot when I was young, but later I realized she had demonstrated her love for us in other ways. She put discipline in our lives. She emphasized getting an education. She introduced us to a spiritual side of life and gave us hope.

My mother did her best at everything she did, and on her level, she excelled. She raised our standard of living all by herself. We went from way below the poverty line to where we at least had the necessities to survive day to day. That may not sound like much of a difference, but believe me, it was.

Some people seem to think success means being rich or having a lot of material possessions. But if you start out real low on the scale, success means not being in the same position you were ten or fifteen years earlier. Mother moved us up.

I remember when we lived off of welfare checks that Mommy received on the 1st and 15th of every month. Welfare checks and food stamps—that was it. Then Mommy realized that wasn't going to cut it and we would be a lot worse off if she continued along those lines. So, on her own, she found herself a job and then took on a second job.

Working two jobs, one of them on the graveyard shift that kept her away from home all night, she was able to give us more: More lunch money. More school supplies. More clothes. More food.

These changes didn't happen overnight; they stretched over a number of years. But my mother would not be denied. She worked her way up to better-paying jobs with better benefits, including health coverage. She did all this for her children. We were her motivation, and she never lost sight of it.

My mother is an inspiring, loving and passionate woman. She's a great lady. Now that I'm playing professionally in the

WNBA, it's my job to give back to my mother and allow her to be her true self.

My brothers and sisters and I didn't always get to see her nurturing qualities when we were younger. My mother had so much pressure on her to make ends meet, she didn't have as much time to spend with us as she would have liked.

It's wonderful to see those great qualities of hers shine through now that she doesn't face the pressure of being the breadwinner.

Our family was devastated when my mother learned she had breast cancer in March 1997. But we felt blessed that I had been assigned to play for the franchise in Houston, which has one of the finest cancer institutions in the world, M.D. Anderson Hospital.

When my mother's cancer was first diagnosed, I remember praying, "Please don't take my mommy, Lord. Don't take her. Because she's my momma. She's the only mother I'm ever going to have."

Then I said to myself, "That's selfish. Whew, is that ever selfish."

So I changed my prayers to ask that the Lord's will be done. If the Lord wants to take my mother home, I can't say I will be okay with that, but at least I'll know she's not suffering any longer.

What we've tried to do is take a negative situation and turn it into a positive one by having my mother share in all the excitement of the WNBA championships the Houston Comets won in 1997 and 1998. I want my mother to enjoy every moment that she's here on earth. That's my focus, no matter how much I have to spend or what I have to do to accomplish that goal.

Since my mother's cancer was detected, we've gone through the usual upheavals during her treatment, all the predictable peaks and valleys. She has always been a very strong woman—motivated, determined and strong-willed. But cancer debilitates an individual. It's such a degenerative disease that it takes away from the physical person and the mental being as well. It strips a person of who they are. I've seen it stripping away at her.

With cancer, fear creeps in, along with uncertainty and unpredictability. People with cancer are uncertain of their future; they sometimes show fear of getting close to you because they might be leaving you soon.

My mother was never the kind of person who gets sick. But now she's sick and that means she has been unable to do some things for herself that she's always been able to do. Just little things, like cooking for herself or going to the supermarket. She's been unable to give her grandchildren all the love and care and attention she gave them right before she got this disease.

It's a dramatic situation, not being able to do the things you're used to doing for your loved ones because of the battle that's waging inside your body. I've seen confusion and doubt in my mother. I've heard uncertainty in her voice.

It's almost like she's become the child and I've become the mother who has to find the right things to say. Now I have to be strong for her, just as she was my strength when I was a shy, confused and uncertain little girl.

During the 1997 season, when my mother was receiving chemotherapy treatment, there were times she was in pain twenty-four hours a day. I remember her having to wake me at 4 A.M. because the pain was so intense. I know she didn't want to get me up at that hour, because I might have practice that day or the Comets might be playing a game that night, but she had no other choice. Her pain was overwhelming.

Sometimes I would massage her arms or legs, or her shoulders, back and neck. Sometimes I would read to her from the

Bible. Sometimes we'd just talk. I did whatever I could to keep her mind off the pain.

No matter how bad she felt, my mother never missed a Houston Comets home game. When we won the first WNBA championship, beating the New York Liberty 65–51 in the championship game at The Summit in Houston, she was right down there on the floor, jumping around and celebrating with us.

The joy on her face was a beautiful sight to see.

Because my mother never missed a game, despite all that was happening to her, I know I will not be stopped by taking a knee in the thigh or getting slammed to the floor when I'm driving to the hoop. I know I'm going to bounce right up and play this game, because compared with what my mother has been through what's a bump or a bruise?

Believe me, it's nothing.

Chapter Three

Hard Times

I've spent years trying to forget many of the painful things that happened to me during my childhood. When a door closes, I try my best to keep it shut.

What I do know is that Mary Cobbs had already given birth to four children, my sisters Joanne and Drena and my brothers Kenny and Everett, when I entered the world on April 14, 1963. It was Easter Sunday.

Mother said she had a quick delivery but a painful one. She said from the beginning I liked to move around a lot. In a sense, I've been running all my life.

When I was barely a year old, my mother moved our family from Chicago, which is where she grew up and where most of her relatives still live, to Los Angeles. She thought the opportunities for work would be better in L.A., and she had heard the school system was better, too.

We moved into government-assisted housing in the South Central area of Los Angeles, what's commonly known as Watts.

About a year later, during August 1965, riots broke out in the neighborhood.

The riots, which were the flashpoint for feelings of hopelessness among the inner-city poor, lasted for six days. The whole area was in a state of civil emergency, and the National Guard had to be called in to restore law and order.

Thirty-four people were killed during the riots, and thousands more were injured. Looting was widespread and cars and buildings were set on fire.

I've heard people say that before the riots, parts of Watts were pretty nice. But afterward, when I was growing up there in the 1970s, Watts had a bunch of empty storefronts with broken glass, littered fields where buildings had once stood and slums in states of disrepair.

Many of the residents of Watts didn't know where their next meal was coming from. The neighborhoods were filthy, with trash lining the streets. Houses had broken windows, torn gutters and peeling paint.

The streets were filled with jobless people, hanging out because they had nowhere else to go, and dirty kids, many without shoes, in need of a bath and shampoo.

We were living below the poverty line. I didn't realize just how poor our family was until I got out in the world and saw what other people had, but even as a kid I knew we didn't have much.

We lived in either small, matchbox houses or cramped, sparsely furnished apartments. There were seven children in our family (Stephanie followed me in 1964 and Lisa in 1967), which meant we never had our own beds, much less our own rooms. I usually shared a bed with Stephanie.

Imagine life with seven kids, two bedrooms and one bathroom. It was crowded, to say the least. And when something around the house broke, we didn't have the money to fix it.

When a bed frame broke, for example, we'd simply put the mattress on the floor and sleep on it.

We didn't have any pets. We could barely feed ourselves, so animals were out of the question. I didn't have a favorite doll, toy or stuffed animal. Sometimes, like on our birthdays, we might get a new toy, but it never was of the best quality so it was hard to keep it intact for long. One year I got a pair of roller skates, but they were so cheap they didn't last.

I never had a bicycle. My brothers and sisters and I walked everywhere we went. I can't remember a favorite or best Christmas gift. We had so little extra money to spend on presents that anything we got for Christmas seemed special.

I never participated in neighborhood youth clubs or organizations like Brownies or Girl Scouts. In the first place, we didn't have the money to join. Besides, that wasn't exactly the mentality where we lived. You don't find many gang members—girls or boys—involved with Scouting.

I wasn't brought up around books or storytelling. No one read to me or my siblings or told us stories. My mother was always too busy working, and my father never seemed to take the time. We didn't watch much television, either, because the TV set usually was broken.

My siblings and I played in the streets, down at the junkyard and on or around the railroad tracks across from our house on Lanzit Avenue. We chased trains, which was both dangerous and stupid, but we didn't know any better. We threw rocks at each other. We played tag.

I also liked to play marbles and jump rope. I claim to be the all-time champion at tether ball.

There were too many of us kids to all hang out together. We didn't move around like a pack. But when we did do things together, Joanne, the oldest child, was the ringleader.

Being something of a tomboy who liked to play sports, I

hung out with my brother Everett, who we called Ricky, more than any of my sisters.

Ricky and I were tight. We were the closest in age—a year apart—and attitude. We shared the goal of getting out of poverty and making something of our lives. We dreamed about one day being able to help Mother with the family bills and expenses.

We played together all the time and protected each other in the neighborhood and at school. We were inseparable. Ricky and I were like two peas in a pod.

One day Ricky and I were playing tag in the junkyard with some of our friends. I was running hard and cut around the corner of a building too sharply. I fell down and scraped up my leg really bad. I still have a scar as a reminder.

Mommy had to take me to the hospital and get me shots to keep the wound from getting infected. I remember her being really mad at me, probably because of the strain my mishap had put on the family budget.

My mother didn't mind paying to have my eyes fixed, though. When I was young, my eyes were slightly crossed, which made me even more self-conscious. I had to start wearing glasses at an early age, about eight or so. I remember having a pair of glasses that looked like cat's eyes. That was a popular style in those days.

Most of the glasses I wore had cheap plastic frames and thick Coke-bottle lenses. For a little girl already self-conscious, having to wear those big, ugly glasses was traumatizing.

My crossed eyes got progressively worse until I needed surgery to correct my vision. When I came home from the hospital, Mommy let me rest in her room.

The doctors had given me a pair of protective shades to wear over my eyes while they healed. They were uncomfortable, so I took them off and tried to get some sleep. Someone came into Mommy's room and flipped on the light switch. Because my eyes were so sensitive to the light, I cried out in pain.

Mommy came running in to see what was wrong, and then yelled at everybody to leave me alone. That made me feel special, because in a family the size of ours, it was rare for anyone to get any individual attention.

What scared me most growing up were the drugs and gangs and overall violence in our neighborhood. I remember walking to the grocery store with my sister Drena one day when I was about eight or nine. I wore a red scarf.

Red happened to be the color of one of the main gangs in Los Angeles, the Bloods. As we were about to enter the store, a boy about sixteen or seventeen started cussing at me. He was a member of a rival gang, the Crips.

Crips wore blue.

He seemed huge. He got in my face and asked me what I was doing, wearing that particular color. I told him my mommy had put it on me to keep my hair in place. He threatened to hurt me, but instead he just snatched the scarf off my head, pulled out a cigarette lighter and set it on fire.

Drena and I didn't wait around to watch the scarf burn. We ran into the store, scared out of our wits. We got what we were looking for and hurried home. We were too terrified to talk about what had happened. We knew it could have been worse.

That incident taught me an important lesson about being careful about the color of clothes you wore around Watts. I realized that colors were a real issue, that gang members took that stuff seriously. If you made a mistake and went on the wrong turf wearing the wrong color, your life could be at risk.

The incident with the member of the Crips reflected the kind of neighborhood we lived in. Walls and buildings in Watts were covered with graffiti and other gang markings. You had to be careful at all times about where you went because you could get hurt for no reason, maybe accidentally hit during a drive-by shooting.

The danger was constant. It never went away. You might be playing hopscotch with your friends outside the projects and suddenly a car would pull around the corner and the guys inside would open fire with automatic or semiautomatic weapons. People dove to the ground or ran away to keep from getting hit.

Or you might be out jumping rope, or practicing your double Dutch, when members of a gang would come down the street and jump on somebody and beat them half to death. Just because they weren't affiliated with that gang.

You never knew when the violence would erupt—only that it would—which made kids feel uneasy when they went outside to play and parents uncomfortable about letting their children go out. People expected the worst and were seldom disappointed.

Besides Ricky, my closest friend growing up was Shearon Bell, who lived next door to us for part of my youth. We were best friends beginning in elementary school and all the way through junior high and high school. She was the one person I could talk with and tell my secrets to—although not all of my secrets. She's always been my girl.

I envied Shearon because she had both parents living at home. It seemed to me like she had the perfect family.

Her house was newer than ours. Her parents' furniture wasn't tattered and beat-up. Shearon always had nice clothes and clean clothes. She didn't wear hand-me-downs. Her family seemed extremely happy and content. What things they needed, they went out and purchased. From my limited perspective, they seemed to have it all.

I told myself that one day I would live like that.

I did very well in school when I was young. Math and science were two of my favorite subjects. English was okay. My school career got off to a rocky start: On the first day of kinder-garten, I ran away. I didn't like being around so many strangers, so when I saw an opportunity to get away, I took it. I thought I could escape, but my teacher ran me down. She must have been pretty quick, because I was a little scooter.

I was the kind of child who never raised her hand to ask the teacher questions and hated to have to get up and read aloud in class. I was timid and scared. I was too unsure of myself and uncertain of who I was. I had a complex about being poor and about the way I looked.

I was also hardheaded. When I thought I was right, then no matter what the teacher said, I'd stand by what I'd said. That's just how it was.

Sports made me happy at school. They became an outlet for the frustrations I had with our situation, and they allowed me to feel equal to other people.

I liked playing softball and volleyball, and I was a terror at kickball. Because I was fast enough to get on base and run around the bases, boys at school always picked me for their team. That was unusual.

I always did well in races we had at 118th Street Elementary School. I ran sprints and relays, and by the time I was in the fifth and sixth grades, I was one of the fastest girls in school, if not the fastest.

During the 1998 WNBA season, when the Houston Comets were in Los Angeles to play the Sparks, I heard some fan shout out during the warm-ups, "Hey, 118th Street Pirates!" I looked up in the stands and saw Mike Natelson, who had been a teacher and coach at our elementary school.

That was pretty cool.

One of the things I remember most clearly about my child-hood is being hungry. I was always hungry. Ricky and I used to stand outside a liquor store in the neighborhood and beg for nickels. On a good day, we might make 50 cents, which was a lot of money for us. We'd take that change and go to the grocery store and buy candy or something else to eat.

There was also a period when we stole food—snacks, chips, sweets—from the same liquor store. I was the fastest runner, so I'd race in the store, grab the food and then dash out. I was really quick. Looking back, I realize the store owner knew we were hungry kids so he let us get away with it.

In a home where food is scarce, there's always a race to the kitchen. No one had to announce "It's time to eat" because the minute the food was ready my brothers and sisters would appear instantaneously, like magic.

Whatever we had to eat was always good and always gone.

We never sat down as a family and ate meals together. Someone would grab a plate and go off to do homework, or they'd go into the living room and watch TV—if the set was working. It wasn't until I went to Spain and Italy many years later that I learned from families there that meals are supposed to be a shared experience. That's when you can sort out the problems of the day or brainstorm or just spend time together.

I learned at an early age to hate potatoes and rice. It seemed like all we ate growing up were pinto beans, rice and potatoes. Especially potatoes, because they were so cheap.

We ate baked potatoes. Sliced potatoes. Round-cut potatoes. French fries. Mashed potatoes. Potatoes with cole slaw. For breakfast, we ate hash browns.

We ate potatoes in so many ways, I thought I was growing up to be a spud.

We would go to the grocery store and buy a 100-pound bag of potatoes and bring it home in a pushcart. Ricky, Stephanie and I would take turns pushing the cart. We liked to make a game of it; sometimes one of us would jump in the cart and get a free ride.

Trust me, 100 pounds of potatoes is a lot of potatoes. It means you never run out. Never.

When we weren't eating potatoes, we were eating rice. We had rice with pinto beans. Rice with gumbo. Rice for breakfast. Rice casserole for dinner.

To wash down all the starches we were putting into our bodies, we drank gallons and gallons of Kool-Aid. Orange, strawberry, cherry, lemon, lime—we drank every flavor Kool-Aid made.

I remember my little sister Lisa would put way too much sugar in the Kool-Aid. It tasted so horrible, we finally stopped letting her make it. Looking back, I think Lisa may have put in too much sugar just to get out of that chore.

With Mother out of the home working most of the time, my older sisters, Joanne and Drena, did most of the cooking. I never got involved with that. My older sisters assumed that a girl who was so gung ho about playing sports had no business being in the kitchen. So while I had to eat potatoes and rice all the time, I never had to prepare them. (I think I reached my thirties before they let me cook a meal for the family.)

My mother was the disciplinarian in our house. Her word was law. She set the rules, one of which was we had to do our homework and our chores before we could even begin to think about going outside to play.

Mother took us to church each Sunday. She introduced us to the Lord and made sure we said our prayers. She taught us that the Lord would help us on any journey we made.

I remember when I was really young, my mother drank a lot and smoked a lot, but one day she stopped doing those things. She had found Jesus and she decided to give her life to the Lord. He gave her the strength to make such a big change in her life.

I'd have to say the best part of my childhood was the time I spent playing with Ricky. He and I were a lot alike. We could look at each other and know exactly what the other person was thinking and feeling. The worst part was the way a few other men in my life treated me. They caused me a lot of pain and harm and left me reeling with doubts about my self-worth.

Chapter Four

Our Little Secret

I wish I had happy memories of my father, Kenny Cooper, but I don't.

I hope he tickled me, cuddled me, bounced me on his knee, held my hand as we walked down the street together, calmed me when I was frightened and rocked me to sleep when I was tired.

I hope he told me that he loved me.

Big Kenny, as he was called, moved out of the house and out of our lives when I was only five or six years old. I didn't see or hear from him again until more than a decade later, during my senior year in high school.

In between, I received no phone calls or letters. No Christmas cards or birthday gifts. All I got from him was silence.

So, in addition to all the shyness, awkwardness and uncertainty I felt as a little girl, I had to grow up a lot without my daddy.

His absence from our family made me feel inadequate and

not worthy to be loved. It contributed to my feeling like a mis-fit, an outcast. It gave me more of a complex about myself.

I remember my daddy being pretty strict with us about chores. Stuff like taking out the trash or cleaning things up, he could have done himself.

I don't think Big Kenny talked to any of us so much as he barked orders: Clean this room. Sweep this floor. Take out the trash. Wash the dishes. Bring me this. Bring me that. Shut your mouth.

Big Kenny didn't play favorites, though. He dogged all of us equally. And if we didn't respond quickly enough, well, let's just say he was a strict disciplinarian. We always hoped that Mom would intervene, but she was so busy working, trying to make money to keep the family going, that many times she just wasn't there. Big Kenny would sit at home and boss us around a lot.

Kenny Cooper may have been called Big Kenny but that was only to differentiate between him and my oldest brother, Kenny.

Big Kenny wasn't all that big. He was no more than 5-foot-9 and roughly 150 pounds. Of course, when you're only four or five years old, every adult male appears as gigantic and over-whelming as Wilt Chamberlain or Kareem Abdul-Jabbar.

If there's one thing my brother Kenny learned from Big Kenny, it was how to bully the entire household, including Ricky, who would try to stand up for us.

There were times Kenny would come home cussing and fussing and start in on all of us. You never knew what would set Kenny off, either.

A few years after Big Kenny moved out, I encountered an-other man—an acquaintance of the family—who had a drink-ing problem.

I don't know what made him do what he did to me. It was

a hot and humid summer day, the kind where sweat sticks to your brow and lip and your clothes feel damp.

To beat the heat, I went with my sisters to a public swimming pool. Some of the tiles around the pool were cracking, but the water was cool and that's all we cared about.

We jumped in. We swam and splashed around, frolicking like kids without a care in the world.

When we came home that afternoon, this man got me alone. He started talking to me with an odd manner and in a strange voice. "Oh, baby, you're so pretty," he cooed. "Come over here and let me get a good look at you. Come on."

Like a good girl, I went over and stood beside him and he hoisted me up on his lap. He'd been drinking and his breath smelled awful.

He touched my face and hair, whispering words of reassurance, calling me a precious girl. I wallowed in his sweet praise.

Then he touched my shoulders and slowly began to lower the right strap of my bathing suit, which left the upper part of my chest exposed. He moved his head down to my breast and started kissing and licking, making an odd noise.

This violation of my body lasted only a minute or two. Maybe he was startled by the sound of a car passing by.

He replaced the strap on my shoulder, lifted me up and put me down on the floor. "That will be our little secret, baby," he told me, waving me away.

I didn't know what to think, other than that something terrible had just happened. I don't remember if I started to cry, but I do recall feeling so dirty all over that no amount of soap and hot water could begin to make me feel clean.

It was a humiliating experience. Filthy, yucky, horrible, awful. I scrubbed and scrubbed as hard as I could.

Later that day the telephone rang. It was him.

"Remember, we have a little secret that's just between us," he told me.

I said okay—even though I knew somehow that it wasn't okay. Not then, not ever.

The man forced himself on me one other time that same summer. This time, he didn't stop his advances at my upper body. He reached under the skirt I was wearing. When he touched me down there, I cried out in pain. The sound must have snapped him out of his alcoholic haze. He came to his senses and quickly removed his hand.

Never again did I let myself get caught alone with him. I stayed out of his way. Whenever I encountered him without other people around, I scooted away faster than Wilma Rudolph or Evelyn Ashford.

Being violated like that leaves its mark. It makes you feel that you mean nothing to anyone. I was already self-conscious about a lot of things—myself, my body, my clothing, who I was, what I represented—including the fact that we were poor.

But this experience was worse than all those feelings combined. It was totally degrading, and it took me to an all-time low. I reached a depth I had never experienced and never thought I would experience.

I felt used and worthless.

A decade passed before I could summon enough courage to tell my mother that I had been molested.

Her first reaction was shock. She had no idea what I had been through. She comforted me and told me how sorry she felt for what had happened.

Her second reaction was anger. She called the man, demanding his explanation for what had occurred.

When my mother spoke to him, I thought he might try to deny everything. I grabbed the phone and said, "Are you going to sit there and say these things never happened?"

"No, no. I'm not denying it," he said. "I'm just saying that I was drunk. I didn't know what I was doing."

He tried to use the excuse that he'd been drunk, but he had made me feel like an object, a piece of meat. He had robbed me of my innocence at a time in my life when innocence was one of the few things I owned.

I developed a genuine dislike for men in those early years of my life. I probably had reason to hate them. The only male I trusted, or felt close to, was Ricky.

By the time I got to high school, I finally came to the realization that I couldn't blame all men for all the bad things that had been done to me.

Chapter Five

Hoping for a Better Life

I suffered from low self-esteem and a lack of self-confidence for many years after being molested. That man's violation of my body made me feel useless, used and dirty. I felt like I was worth nothing at all.

I lived alone with my pain and hurt, unable to tell anyone what had happened. I couldn't tell my mother, because she had enough problems just trying to keep our family together and make ends meet.

I couldn't tell my older sisters or brothers. I didn't feel close enough to Joanne or Drena. I wasn't about to tell Kenny or Ricky. Besides, they were probably all too young to understand.

I couldn't tell my best friend, Shearon, because I was too ashamed and embarrassed. I didn't want Shearon to know what terrible things were going on in our house, especially because I believed she had a perfect family.

I got to be pretty good at hiding my true feelings in the

years that followed. I tried to fake like everything was normal and okay, even though I knew it wasn't.

But as much as you fake and pretend, trying to make people think you're confident, the real person inside you is just this scared child who believes she has no rightful place in this world.

I retreated into my own little protective shell. I felt like I was the only person in the world being forced to suffer through such a terrible fate.

Many nights I cried myself to sleep. I did my best to muffle the sounds so my sisters couldn't hear. Or I'd get up and go into the bathroom. I'd look in the mirror and see this pitiful, worthless creature. I'd start to bawl.

Sometimes I cried because I didn't have the kind of relationship I wanted with my mother. There were many times she came home from work so worn out and irritable that she couldn't give us the attention we needed. That made me sad.

I cried over feeling lonely and because I didn't have anyone to share my feelings with, not even Shearon or Ricky. I cried over things we didn't have. I cried because I felt inferior to everyone else on earth. I cried because I didn't have anyone in my life to encourage me or make me feel wanted.

In those days I went through many rolls of toilet paper just wiping away tears.

Somehow, though, I managed to keep the bad things that had happened to me from touching my soul and breaking my spirit. I wouldn't let feelings of hatred and hostility get inside me and grow like a cancer. It took many years, but I finally accepted what had happened to me and tried my best to move on. Coming to terms with the pain was difficult, but doing so allowed the scars to heal.

I didn't reach this level of awareness and understanding, which allowed me to put the past behind, until I was around thirty years old. Back in my teenage years, with the memories of abuse still fresh and vivid, I was filled with confusion and pain.

During those years in junior high and high school, even with all the bad things going on in my life, I began dreaming about better days ahead. I clung to the hope that somewhere on the horizon was a better life than the one I'd known up to that point.

Mommy had instilled in me a belief that the Lord has a plan for each of us and that if I would keep my faith and trust in Jesus Christ, I would be rewarded. I had no idea what plans the Lord had for my future, but I anticipated happier days. My prayers filled me with hope.

One thing holding back many of the inner-city kids like me was the lack of positive role models. I didn't know as a teenager what I was going to become. I didn't dream of being a doctor, lawyer, teacher or a professional basketball player, much less a two-time Olympian and WNBA star.

People at our level couldn't even imagine such things. We were just living day to day. Trying to get by as best we could.

While I didn't know what I wanted to become, I had definite ideas about what I didn't want to be. Because of the environment we lived in, with all the negative examples at every turn, I knew exactly what I didn't want to have happen in my life.

I didn't want to be one of the kids who dropped out of school because the work was too hard or because going to school wasn't as cool as doing drugs or being a gang member. I didn't want to be involved with drugs or gangs, period. I didn't want to have a baby at age fifteen or sixteen.

I didn't have any positive role models—other than my mother—but I had plenty of examples of what I shouldn't become. People didn't have to explain to me that drugs would kill; I saw it every day. People didn't have to explain that teen pregnancy meant dropping out of school and drug addiction;

I was living with it. People didn't have to explain about abusive relationships; I saw them.

I knew what drugs could do to your body, your family, your life and future. I saw it every day in school, on TV, sometimes in my house. Everywhere I turned, I saw twenty examples of what I shouldn't do.

I didn't know I had the opportunity to be a success because I had so many examples of failure all around me. There were no role models, other than people who showed me what not to do. But I believed there was something better in life than what I saw on the streets every day.

I could see that on the television. I could read about it in the newspaper. I knew the harsh and bitter world we lived in wasn't the only one available.

When I began competing in athletics in high school, I traveled with my teams to other neighborhoods and school districts. I got to see and meet kids who were happy, kids who were excited about their lives. These kids had a future. They weren't headed down a dead-end street. They had places to go and plans for how to get there.

Seeing them motivated me to have the same kind of experiences. I became determined to be like them.

What I wanted to be was an educated woman. I wanted to go to school and take care of my business in the classroom. I wanted to get an education and become a successful person.

I saw examples in Watts every day of people who didn't take that same stance about education. Every day I saw people who had succumbed, who had given in to the situation and given up their hopes and dreams. They were victims of their environment.

Even though I remained an awkward and timid teenager who kept mostly to herself, I began to tell myself that I would get out of the negative environment I found myself in. And when I did get out, I made a promise not to become involved in an abusive relationship, where either the husband beat the wife or the boyfriend beat the girl. I'd seen enough violence against women already.

While I held on to my dreams of a brighter future, reality interfered. We were living on Lanzit Avenue in Watts. I was sitting up alone late one night, watching TV, when I got out of bed to get a drink in the kitchen.

I opened the bedroom door and knew immediately something was wrong. I smelled smoke. There were no lights on in the hallway, so everything was dark, but I could make out a thick layer of black smoke curling up along the ceiling.

I ran into the kitchen, where the fire had started. Then I raced back down the hall screaming as loud as I could, waking up everyone in the house.

The interior starting burning fast. Bright, angry flames shot up like walls, blocking off escape routes through the living room and kitchen. The thick smoke worked its way down from the ceiling like a dense black cloud. We were all choking and coughing, trying to cover our mouths to keep from inhaling too much smoke.

I finally hopped out the window in our bedroom, and Stephanie handed me our little half brother, Chucky, who was just a baby. She followed me out.

Everyone in our family escaped unharmed, but by the time fire trucks pulled up and got the hoses going, our house was pretty much a total loss. Between the smoke and water damage, we salvaged only a few possessions. And they were all sooty and smoke-damaged.

The fire officials wrote up the report as an electrical fire. We never found out for certain how it got started, whether the source was a faulty plug or bad wiring.

The experience taught me a lesson about why people buy

homeowner's insurance. Unfortunately, my mother couldn't afford any, so she was unable to recover any of our loss.

I remember the Lanzit fire being a really sad time in our lives. My mother already had a lot of pressure on her and now this. That night she sat up for hours sobbing, "What am I going to do? How am I going to make ends meet? Where are we going to live?"

As low as our family had been on the economic ladder, the fire knocked us down a couple more rungs. We'd been poor before, but now we started living real bad.

Mommy had to move us into a small three-bedroom apartment near the Jordan Downs projects at 105th and Lou Dillon. Our apartment was one of four units in an off-white building with brown trim and graffiti-covered walls. It was a dreary place. I remember the screen door had broken hinges and was filled with holes. Not that we had many visitors.

This was deep, deep Watts, a really dangerous environment. We heard shooting every night. Every single night. Guys were hanging out all day on street corners—every corner—and at the liquor store. Prostitutes worked the streets with impunity. Drug deals regularly went down on every corner of the block.

The neighborhood was so tough, Mother made a rule that we had to be in the house by sundown. In that environment, you didn't want to be out at night if you didn't have to.

My mother went through the Salvation Army to get us some secondhand furniture and secondhand clothes to wear. Our church, the Crenshaw Christian Center, chipped in with food and household supplies. She immediately began working extra hours to get us out of the projects as fast as she could.

About my only pleasant memory about living near Jordan Downs is that the lady who lived next door baked coffee cakes every morning. She sold pieces for a dime. Man, I couldn't wait until she finished baking those coffee cakes. You could smell them all the way down the street.

There was also a small store at the end of the corner that only sold candy. That was it, nothing but candy. That was some kind of store; I wish I had a franchise for it.

We stayed in that apartment for nearly two years. During that time my mother worked two jobs, day and night, to get us out of there as fast as she could.

One day she came home and said she was buying a house. She took us over to see it, and I remember walking with her around the outside of the property and saying several prayers.

We prayed that her loan application would be approved. We prayed that nothing bad—like a fire—would happen when we moved in. Those were answered prayers because my mother completed the transaction and we had ourselves a new home.

The house wasn't located in a great neighborhood, but it was an improvement from where we'd been. The family was making progress, we were getting back on track.

My mother had done it again. She had somehow found a way for us to have a better life.

Chapter Six

Finding My Gift

The same year the fire drove us from the house on Lanzit and relocated us near the Jordan Downs projects, I discovered my gift: playing basketball.

I remember sitting in the gym at Gompers Junior High one day in the spring of 1978. I watched a girl dribbling a basketball go in for a layup. She swung the ball around behind her back before kissing it off the backboard and into the hoop.

"Wow," I said to myself, "that looks pretty cool. I'd like to learn to do that myself."

I didn't know the first thing about how to play basketball, but I was acquainted with Lucias Franklin, who was one of the assistant coaches at Locke High School, where I was scheduled to enroll the following fall.

I asked him to show me how to play. He told me he didn't have time, he was too busy. I kept pestering him. He told me to wait until school started up again. I wouldn't give up, though. I called him at home, begging and pleading with him.

Lucias Franklin finally succumbed to my persuasiveness. That summer, he met me every day at Locke High and started teaching me the fundamentals of basketball. He showed me how to dribble the ball with my right hand and with my left. He showed me how to hold the ball when you shoot, cradling it with your fingertips and keeping it out of the palm, and how to get into a defensive posture and shuffle your feet.

I was a fast learner. By the time tryouts took place that fall, I had developed enough game—or at least showed enough potential—to make the varsity team at Locke High.

I broke into the starting lineup as a sophomore. I was as skinny as a No. 2 pencil, but I possessed good speed and with my height (5-foot-8), I became a demon at grabbing rebounds. My skills as a ball handler and shooter steadily improved.

Locke High's head girls coach was Art Webb. Coach Webb, who also taught science, was a disciplinarian and motivator. He didn't get involved with the strategy of the game all that much. He put the pieces in place and then let Lucias Franklin, his assistant, make them work.

Coach Webb's primary concern was making sure all his players were going to class and getting an education. Once he realized we had the chance to excel and become a championship team, he began working us really hard. He helped instill the strong work ethic I've had throughout my career.

My first experience in organized sports taught me some of the value of athletics. Besides good conditioning and a healthier lifestyle, athletics is a vehicle that girls can use to develop confidence in themselves and build character. Athletics equips a person with the determination to succeed and excel.

Girls develop better people skills by playing team sports, and they learn how to interact in group settings. They also learn about setting goals—team and individual. Team sports has taught me a lot of lessons about life and continues to teach me important lessons to this very day. I wouldn't be the same person I am without embracing my gift.

Beginning the summer after my sophomore year, I began to spend as much time on the basketball court as I possibly could. I played on the outdoor courts at Locke High, with the chain nets and the wooden backboard with the faded square above the rim.

Ricky and I went up there one afternoon that summer, and I beat him in a game of one-on-one. I wore him out. He came home and started whining about what had happened, and my mother made us march right back up to the school. She insisted that I let him beat me, so I did.

It had something to do with male pride and ego. Still, I didn't think that was fair.

I started playing more and more with guys, which told me my game was improving. Guys will never let a girl play in their game unless she can hold her own. Then it's okay.

My junior year, the Locke High Saints had a winning record and advanced to the first round of the state playoffs. We let our hair grow out naturally, and our mini-Afros resembled the style made popular by NBA players like Julius Erving and Larry Kenon.

We might have advanced further in the playoffs that year, but the night before the playoff game, Kenny came home cussing and fussing. It never took much to set my brother off, and he started in on me, my mother and some of my siblings.

That happened on several different occasions. Kenny would go off on us, and after these episodes I didn't have much energy left to put into any basketball game. It really got to me. I was exhausted by what had happened the previous night, and I couldn't keep my mind off what might happen to us that night after the game if Kenny went off again.

I played poorly and missed a lot of shots. We lost.

My success in high school sports—track as well as basketball—had started to give me a little bit of self-confidence. I realized that I might be able to use athletics as a means of getting a college scholarship. I knew that would be the only way I could afford to go.

The possibility of a scholarship got my mother's attention, too. She never seemed all that excited when I started playing basketball at Locke High—even though she had played basketball herself in Chicago when she was growing up. (Mother played in the days when women's basketball was a six-player game, three on offense and three on defense. She played on offense and likes to say I inherited my jump shot from her.)

She told me if it came down to daily chores or basketball, my chores would prevail. End of discussion. Early on when I started playing at Locke, she forced me to miss a lot of practices—which upset Coach Webb a great deal—because the house wasn't clean or the dishes weren't washed.

I think my older sisters started to slough off doing their own chores once they realized how passionate I was about playing basketball. They figured I would do their chores as well as my own, just so the house would be clean and I could leave for practice.

Despite our team's success in basketball, I didn't feel like anything special, though. I still battled an inferiority complex. I thought I was ugly and dorky and not part of the in crowd.

Shearon Bell and I were still best friends. When I ran away from home one time after a big family argument, I went straight to Shearon's house because that was the safest place I could think of. I stayed one night.

Mother tracked me down by telephone and told me to get my butt back home. I stayed that one night at Shearon's, went to school the next day and then went home. I thought for sure I was going to get a whipping, but for some reason I didn't. All was forgotten and forgiven.

Shearon and I hung around together at school, eating

lunch every day in the cafeteria. The other basketball players didn't want us hanging around with them because we didn't have boyfriends. They didn't think we were cool.

The summer between my junior and senior year, Shearon's mother would sometimes drive us over to Venice Beach. Shearon would want to just hang out, but I'd wind up getting into pickup basketball games with guys. The competition at the beach made me a better player.

Something else happened that year. When you're in a gang-infested, drug-infested neighborhood, a lot of people are jealous of your success. But there's a funny thing, almost like an unspoken rule: The gang members will protect you if they see you have a chance to get out.

Once I started having some success in basketball, I no longer felt the pressure to get involved with gangs or drugs. People that did those things started to stay away from me. All of a sudden, they left me alone.

My last year of high school, with an experienced group of players, Locke High won the 1981 California 4A state championship. The Saints had a starting lineup of JaDon Armstrong, Taja Winston, Regina Myles, Andrea Anthony and me.

We were fast and aggressive and used our quickness and athleticism to push the pace. We created a lot of easy baskets off turnovers. Coach Webb kept us motivated. Coach Franklin pushed the right buttons and we did the rest.

Our team uniforms were sky blue and gold. We had an outstanding season, and we had a lot of fun. We played the game for sheer enjoyment, not because we thought it was a life-or-death proposition. In some situations, parents and coaches put so much pressure on their children to win that they take all the fun out of the competition. High school sports aren't meant to be that way.

For the championship game, we flew up to Oakland—probably the first time I'd ever been out of greater Los Angeles and definitely my first trip on an airplane—and beat a team from Northern California called Live Oak.

Before we made that trip to the finals, we went to the mall and bought some lettering to put on our warm-up suits. Andrea Anthony, our floor leader and the most popular player on the team, was "The Magician." I became "The Wizard." We had a speedy substitute player named Kim Huey who became "The Rabbit." We thought we were hot stuff with those warm-up suits.

That season I averaged 31 points a game and was named the Marine League's MVP and the Los Angeles City Player of the Year. As I recall, I scored 45 points in one game, which might have set a school record.

One of the L.A. TV stations sent a crew out to Locke after we won the state championship. They focused much of the segment on me. It was a big thrill to see myself on television and hear myself talking. The interview happened so fast, I have no idea what I said. (I ran into the TV reporter who did the piece during the 1998 WNBA season. "I thought I went out there to do a story on a team," he told me, "but I wound up doing a story on you.")

The publicity had immediate repercussions. The next day at school, I was in the middle of a debate in government class when someone from the office interrupted and said I had an important telephone call. I forget the exact topic we were debating, but I know I was winning. I know it.

I went running to the office, thinking something bad must have happened to my mother or one of my siblings. I wasn't prepared for the shock I got when I picked up the receiver.

"Do you know who this is?" said a stranger's voice.

"No," I replied.

"It's Big Kenny. Your daddy. I'm proud of you, girl."

Hearing his voice again after so many years threw me for a loop. I was stunned.

Big Kenny wanted to see me again. I admit I was curious about seeing him, too. So we arranged for me to pay him a visit. He lived in the Crenshaw area of Los Angeles, not far from Watts. By then he had remarried and had three sons.

The boys were about fifteen, eleven and eight. When I got to Big Kenny's house, I noticed right away the three boys talked back to him and their mother. When we sat down to eat, I was shocked to see their table manners. I looked over at my daddy; I couldn't figure out why someone as bossy and demanding as Big Kenny would let his sons behave like that. It didn't make any sense.

At the end of the school year, shortly before graduation, I attended the senior prom. I guess some high school girls look forward to their prom, but I dreaded going.

I wasn't sure if I wanted to attend. Beyond that was the issue of finding an escort. I was eighteen years old and I had never been out on a date. Not one.

I got a date for the prom with Terry Brisco. Terry ran on the Locke track team and was a good athlete. His older sister, Valerie Brisco-Hooks, would become a two-time gold medal winner at the 1984 Olympic Games in Los Angeles.

I got to dress up in formal wear for the first time, and I felt like someone special. I wore lavender flowers in my hair and a sheer lavender shawl over my white gown, which had a hoop skirt. I was jamming. Or at least I thought I was.

Terry was a real gentleman. He was serious, sensitive and intelligent. He reminded me a lot of my brother Ricky. Not in looks or anything, but in his kindness and thoughtfulness. Terry, like my brother, had a great sense of humor and was easy to talk to.

At the prom, Terry and I danced, had our pictures taken and socialized with our classmates. Then we went home, got out of all those uncomfortable clothes and went to the after-party, which was a big dance. That was a lot more fun.

For a girl who had never dated, I could hold my own on the dance floor. I taught myself to dance in front of a mirror at home, listening to Jackson 5 records.

When you learn that way, you don't have anyone saying that you're no good. No one criticizes you or gives you a hard time or says you're doing this or that the wrong way.

You just turn that music on and everything is all right.

Locke's state championship run and my individual success had attracted the attention of college recruiters. I started receiving letters and phone calls at home.

I was excited and thrilled beyond belief. So was my mother. For the first time, college no longer seemed like an impossible dream for me.

I had figured I'd have to find a job immediately after high school and begin to start saving money; maybe in a few years I would have enough to start college. Because of basketball, though, everything had suddenly changed; for the first time, it looked like I had a real future. I knew I could get an education and someone was willing to pay for it.

Several college coaches wanted me to pay a visit to their campuses, but we didn't have the money for me to make any visits outside the immediate area. (Back then, colleges couldn't pick up the expenses when a recruit came for an official visit; nowadays, they can.)

I didn't want to stray far from home anyway, so I narrowed my choices to the University of California at Los Angeles and the University of Southern California, both in Los Angeles. USC seemed to want me pretty bad, but UCLA didn't recruit me very hard. That was okay, I was leaning to USC. By then, I had taken a real liking to head coach Linda Sharp.

Coach Sharp, who had taken over the Lady Trojans in the

1977–78 season, was putting together a strong program. Her 1981 team had won 26 games and advanced to the AIAW (Association for Intercollegiate Athletics for Women) Final Four.

"We have the McGee twins coming back," she told me, although I was too embarrassed to tell Coach Sharp I didn't know the McGee twins from the Pointer Sisters. I didn't follow women's college basketball closely, if at all.

I signed a letter of intent with USC shortly after the state championship game. Coach Sharp came over to Locke High and I signed the papers while my mother, as well as Art Webb and Lucias Franklin, looked on. It was one of the happiest days of my life.

But my athletic career at Locke High wasn't over. After basketball season, I joined the track team. I put these long legs of mine to good use, winning the 400 meters, my favorite event, in several meets.

I liked to stride the first 250 meters, then accelerate around the final turn and blaze down the straightaway. I know Michael Johnson would have been proud of me.

My best event in track, though, was the 300-meter low hurdles. That race combines strength and stamina with technique. I won the Los Angeles city championship and at one point that season had the fastest time in the entire nation.

I suppose it's appropriate that I would do so well running the hurdles. If there's one thing my life illustrates it's this:

Put an obstacle in front of me and I'll overcome it.

Chapter Seven

Culture Shock

I was signed, sealed and delivered to the University of Southern California. Then in the summer of 1981, before enrolling for my freshman year, I accompanied Linda Sharp to the Jones Cup, an international basketball competition, which was taking place in Taipei, Taiwan.

One of the players originally selected for the U.S. team had been injured, which opened up a spot on the roster. Coach Sharp probably thought I could use some seasoning, so she asked me to fill in.

I had just tried out for the U.S. Sports Festival team in Northern California and had been the last player cut. Always looking for the opportunity to play more ball, I accepted Coach Sharp's invitation. I didn't have a passport and I didn't know where my birth certificate was, but I knew I wanted to have this new experience. We got all the necessary papers in order, and I was on my way.

Most of the other players on America's Jones Cup team already had played a year or two of college ball, meaning I was the youngest player on the squad. Also the most scared and intimidated.

When I got to Taiwan with my coach and teammates, I suffered a case of culture shock. I couldn't get over how many people were crammed into such a small space in Taiwan, riding bicycles and darting all over the place. I decided to stay in the team's hotel as much as I could.

I didn't speak the language, of course, and I didn't know what to eat. I was so afraid of Taiwanese food that I didn't eat anything for the first two days we were there. For someone as skinny (roughly 130 pounds) as I was, that was risky. I couldn't afford to lose any weight.

Instead of spending my per diem on food or to buy some souvenirs, I used it to call home every day. Hearing the sound of my mother's voice calmed me down and let me know everything was all right.

As intimidated as I was in Taiwan—the U.S. team finished runner-up to the team from China—I remember thinking on the plane ride coming back that the trip had been a positive experience. I considered it a stepping-stone that would help get me ready for college.

But the culture shock I experienced in Taiwan was nothing compared with what I felt my freshman year.

The USC campus sits in the middle of Los Angeles, just a few miles up a freeway from Watts, but it might as well have been on a different continent. Nothing I saw on the campus, from the clean buildings to the lush landscaping, looked anything like the drab environment where I'd grown up. It was like another world.

Mama drove me up to the USC campus that first morning in her beat-up Ford Pinto station wagon, the one with a broken windshield, chipped paint, wheezing engine and coughing muffler.

We puttered to a stop in front of the dorm I'd been assigned to and found ourselves surrounded by a fleet of Benzes, BMWs, Jaguars and other imported luxury cars I couldn't even recognize. I remember seeing one USC student step out of a limousine that had chauffeured her to campus.

I could tell right away that my classmates were on a whole different level. They were so far out of my league I considered looking for a back door to enter the dorm.

It took some USC students an hour or more to unload all their personal possessions. Kids living in my dorm brought in racks and racks of clothes, stereo systems with speakers, TV sets, personal computers, hot plates and popcorn makers and enough cosmetics to open a store—the works.

Me? All my worldly possessions were packed in two suitcases and a hanging bag. Mommy carried my gym bag, filled with sneakers, shorts and sweats. It took us about two minutes to unload the Pinto and move me into the dorm.

I was miserable right from the start. All my anxieties about being poor and inferior started rising up. I didn't have anything against anybody, it's just that I didn't have any idea how to relate to the other students. I didn't know how to socialize or coexist with these people.

Because I felt so inferior to everyone around me, I began copping an attitude. I started acting like a smart aleck. I mouthed off, wouldn't listen to anyone and did things my own way, even if I knew it was the wrong thing to do.

All my actions were just a defense mechanism to mask my true feelings. I really felt like I had nothing in common with the other students—black, white, Asian—when, in fact, I had everything in common with them. Only I couldn't recognize or accept that; I really thought I wasn't worthy to be there. When I found out it cost $20,000 a year to go to school at USC, I *knew* I was unworthy. I didn't have the same status as those other kids.

I had a particularly difficult time relating to white students. I'd never had a single white friend in my life. I think there were only two white kids at Locke High when I was going there, and I never met either one of them.

Up to that point, based on my limited experience growing up in the inner city, I equated white people with success and black people with failure. That's not right—it's totally unfair—but that was all I knew. Being around so many white kids on campus and in the dorm reinforced my feelings of failure. I got hung up on racial generalizations.

The first white friend I made was Tracy Longo, another freshman basketball player. Tracy had been a big star coming out of high school in San Gabriel, California, where she'd been named to several All-America teams. Tracy, a six-foot blonde, was outgoing and full of energy and enthusiasm. She possessed a great sense of humor. She was always smiling and making people laugh.

Early that first semester at USC, Tracy talked me into going with her to a rock concert on campus. It was more culture shock.

Let me first say I wasn't a fan of rock music. R&B was my thing. I like music mellow and full of soul—not just a bunch of power chords on electric guitars.

I couldn't get into the scene at the concert. The whole thing blew me away. The band was loud and the white kids were jumping around like they really enjoyed it. Wow, I thought, this is really amazing.

I wasn't having any fun, and because I seemed to be the only person not enjoying myself or the music, I slipped away from Tracy and the others and went back to my room.

I remember telling Coach Sharp that fall that the transition out of the ghetto was proving too difficult for me and that I was going to leave school. I don't think I was really serious about quitting; I was just reaching out for her help.

I felt so alone and overwhelmed, I needed her help to understand my feelings and to explain to me that my situation would improve.

I also told Coach Sharp I wanted out of the dorm. By then my first roommate had moved out, which left me alone. This was a blessing because I didn't have the pressure of trying to be as good as someone sharing the same space, but I still wasn't happy with the situation.

I begged Coach Sharp to let me move into an apartment near the campus or maybe into another dorm where other USC athletes lived. She wouldn't let me. She wanted me to make an adjustment and learn to coexist with the other kids, both male and female. She wanted me to get over the hump of the first few months.

Another form of culture shock was taking place in the classroom that fall. I immediately discovered that inner-city high schools don't do a very good job of getting kids ready for college. From the beginning at USC, I had to play catch-up in my studies.

The athletic department assigned me tutors and tried to provide all the help it could, but I realized from day one the educational part of my college experience wasn't going to be easy. I was so far behind, I had trouble keeping up.

Gradually, I began to feel more comfortable moving around the campus and meeting other students, many of whom came from lower-class families and were receiving financial aid. Finding out I wasn't the only impoverished kid on campus gave me some comfort and helped put me at ease.

One of the things I began to realize that fall was that at college, everyone has a dream and a focus. Most all of the students are highly motivated and have a plan for success, and you can feed off their energy and purpose.

I also learned that I wasn't the only USC student who was struggling. Everyone struggles to some degree in college. The majority of USC students were struggling to pay for their tuition or books or housing and they were struggling with the same social adjustments I was going through.

In the first few months of my freshman year, the place I felt most comfortable was at the gym, working out with my new Lady Trojan teammates and playing scrimmage games.

On the basketball court, I was in my element. I could hold my own and do my thing. Otherwise, I felt like a fish out of water that first semester at USC, totally out of place.

Fortunately, I met some good role models. Two of the first friends I made at college were the James twins—Ann and Marsha. The twins were regular students, not athletes. They lived in the same dorm as I and we started hanging out.

The James twins were poised, articulate and carried themselves with dignity and class. I watched the graceful manner in which they talked to other students and made new friends. I noticed how they acted without a trace of self-consciousness.

I started turning myself into a sponge, soaking up their every move and action, the same way I would study the moves of basketball players, like the Los Angeles Lakers. Thanks to the James twins, some of my feelings of inferiority began to fade away, though not all of them and not all at once.

Ann and Marsha began rounding out my education in a nonacademic way. They taught me things every woman needs to know. They showed me how to comb my hair and wear it different ways. They helped take some of the street talk out of my speech. They gave me advice on what clothes to wear and some sorely needed sense of fashion.

Whether they realized it or not, the James twins were smoothing off some of my rough edges. They were helping me become a lady.

One time during my freshman year, Ann and Marsha invited me to go home with them for the weekend. Their parents lived in Chino Hills, an hour's drive east of the USC campus, near Pomona.

The James family had a nice ranch-style house with a two-car garage and a manicured lawn. Both of Ann and Marsha's parents lived at home. I thought: So this is what it's like in the rest of the world. When my head hit the pillow that night, I dreamed that someday I might be as lucky as Ann and Marsha.

A couple years later, I took Marsha with me to Watts. I made her sit in my car and wait while I went inside our house to get something. I felt too ashamed to let her see how my family lived and how little we had. It was one of life's embarrassing moments.

Looking back, I realize I was being foolish and immature. But the maturity level of a twenty-one-year-old isn't the highest. I later realized Marsha wouldn't have thought any less of me because of what my family had or didn't have.

Playing in a pickup game at the North Gym that fall, a few weeks before the start of official workouts, I suffered the first injury of my basketball career. It happened when I banged knees with Paula McGee. I was driving to the hoop, and she tried to block me with her leg.

I absorbed the impact of the collision and knew immediately something was wrong with my leg. I limped off the court and went to see the team trainer. The injury, which resulted in some damaged cartilage in my right knee, forced me to undergo arthroscopic surgery and set my progress back several weeks.

The McGee twins, Pam and Paula, were sophomores during the 1981–82 season and had already established themselves as the stars of the Lady Trojans. Each stood 6-foot-3 and both had good all-around skills. The twins had come to USC from Flint, Michigan, in what represented a big recruiting coup for Coach Sharp.

Pam was a bona fide center, who played with her back to

the basket and crashed the boards hard. Paula, who handled the ball better and had a flashier game than her sister, could play either in the post or out on the perimeter.

As freshmen in 1980–81, Paula had averaged 20 points a game and Pam averaged 15. Paula had set a USC single-season record with 683 points and received some All-America mention.

The McGees had charisma and played ball with great flair. Off the court, they were flashy dressers. They looked like they could have been runway models—come to think of it, they did appear as fashion models on one of the L.A. TV stations—or cover girls for *Ebony* or *Essence*.

I considered the McGee twins the perfect example of fierceness on the court and femininity off the court. Naturally, I felt inferior to them.

Compared with the McGees, I was raw and unsophisticated. I was the same person on the court or off the court. If you liked it, fine. If you didn't, tough. That's just the way I was. I didn't bend for anyone or anything. I was wild.

If there was a blessing to the knee injury I suffered that fall, it was my introduction to the first true love of my life, Mark Robins.

Mark, who played wide receiver for the USC football team, was two years older than me and two classes ahead. He had dark skin, a handsome face and wonderful smile. And he had a great sense of humor. He also had a strong, athletic body, and as you might expect for a wide receiver, he had nice hands. Just kidding.

We met in the USC training room. We were both rehabbing knee injuries, although his was more serious than mine. He had hurt his knee playing football at Long Beach City College, but he had so much potential USC gave him a scholarship anyway.

Mark and I became friends at first, and then later we had a deeper relationship that lasted for more than two years. When it ended, I was crushed. I carried a torch for him for another seven or eight years.

That boy took a lot of getting over.

By the time I regained full strength in my knee, the 1981–82 season was already under way. It took me eight games to break into Coach Sharp's starting lineup as the shooting guard.

The McGee twins remained the go-to players for the Women of Troy. Paula and Pam each averaged around 20 points and 10 rebounds a game that year. I finished as the team's third leading scorer, averaging 14.6 for the season and 17.0 in conference games. That performance earned me mention on one of the freshman All-America teams.

A couple of memories stand out from my first year at USC. In early February, we played our archrival, UCLA, on its home court, Pauley Pavilion. I wanted to show the UCLA coach, Billie Moore, that she had made a mistake by not trying to recruit me harder. I didn't feel she had wanted me to play for her, so I had something to prove. I wanted her to see she had missed out on getting a special player.

The UCLA game was broadcast on ESPN, so a national audience saw me lead us to a 97–94 victory by scoring 30 points, a season high. What I never would have guessed at that time was that 30 points would also be my career high at USC.

The win meant a lot to Coach Sharp because Billie Moore had been Linda's college coach at Cal State Fullerton. It meant a lot to me, too, because I had proven my point to Coach Moore. She saw how I could light it up. I was driving to the hoop that night and burying my jump shots. I felt unstoppable.

A couple weeks after the UCLA game, I came through in the clutch against our main competition for the Western Conference Athletic Association title, the Cal State Long Beach 49ers.

The game was played at our home court, the Los Angeles Sports Arena. We were tied 65–65 with under 25 seconds to go. Instead of looking to the McGees, Coach Sharp ran a play for me. I came over the top of a screen and hit a short jumper to win the game.

The loss for Long Beach, despite 29 points by LaTaunya Pollard, one of the sweetest shooters I'd ever played against, was the 49ers' first defeat in conference play. (When we played them again ten days later for the WCAA championship, they beat us 89–84 in three overtimes.)

What was even more special than hitting the jump shot that night was the telephone call I received from Mark Robins in my dorm room. He had come to watch me play for the first time. I remember him saying these exact words: "Cynthia, I am so proud of you."

Wow! That was probably the nicest and sweetest thing I'd ever heard. I couldn't remember anyone ever saying anything like that to me. It blew me away. I wasn't on cloud nine; I was on cloud 1999.

I mean, I loved that guy. He was all that.

Another memory from that first season is less pleasant. After one of our home games, I was standing around visiting with my mother when a USC fan came up and congratulated me on the team's win and my performance. He said, "Hey, I just met your dad and mom. They're really nice people."

Big Kenny and his wife had come to see me play that day. I guessed he was introducing his wife as my mother. Just the thought of it really made me angry, especially when I thought about all the sacrifices Mother had made to help me reach that point and how little my father had contributed. My mother was angry thinking about it, too; neither one of us was thrilled by the thought of Big Kenny's trying to step in and share the glory.

I got so mad that day I haven't spoken to him since. I'm not sure Mother has, either.

The Lady Trojans had been ranked as high as number two in the nation during 1981–82, but we had a bad stretch as the season wore down, losing three of four games, including the WCAA finale to Cal State Long Beach.

We regained momentum at the start of the NCAA playoffs, beating Kent State 99–55 at the Sports Arena in the first round. That win moved us into the Mideast Regional at Knoxville, Tennessee, where we edged Penn State 73–70.

Our season ended with a heartbreaking loss to Tennessee in the Mideast final. The Lady Vols, in front of their huge— 10,000 fans—and vocal home crowd, beat us 91–90. Even though I was disappointed with the loss and determined not to let that happen again, it had been one of the best, most competitive games I'd ever played in. Moments like those made all the hard work worthwhile.

The game was also my first exposure to Tennessee coach Pat Summitt, who has become recognized as one of the premier coaches in the women's game. She was busy in those days building the foundation for her dynasty, which now numbers six NCAA titles, including consecutive NCAA titles in 1996, 1997 and 1998. (Who knows, by the time you read this, she may have added yet another crown.)

What I remember most is that I'd never seen so many people support women's basketball the way the Lady Vols fans did—and continue to do. I thought they were tremendous. I was eager to help build USC into such a great program that people in Los Angeles would follow us with the same intensity and passion.

I had come a long way during my first year at USC. I had been a sponge, trying to soak up new experiences and learn lessons about how to act, talk, carry myself and make new friends.

The McGee twins had given me a push on the court. The James twins had given me direction off the court. Mark Robins had come into my life and given me someone I felt comfortable around. Someone who listened to me, didn't judge and took me for what I was. Success with Lady Trojans basketball had given me more confidence that I had a future in the game.

Despite all the positive things happening, though, I still had a long way to go toward feeling better about who I was.

I couldn't erase in one year all the pain and loneliness I carried with me from Watts. I still had a lot of baggage.

Chapter Eight

Championship Seasons

I thought that during my sophomore season at USC there would be more games like the 30 points I scored as a freshman against UCLA. I was deeply disappointed when there weren't.

My scoring average slipped to 9.5 points a game for the 1982–83 season. My high game was 19 points, in the first round of the NCAA playoffs against Northeast Louisiana. I scored all 19 in the first half, incidentally.

I became less of a force on offense for the Lady Trojans as a sophomore because, in addition to the McGee twins, who were now juniors, Coach Linda Sharp had recruited another big, agile, versatile player: Cheryl Miller.

Cheryl arrived at USC having been the most highly recruited high school player in the United States. She was considered by some experts to be the best player in women's basketball even before she played her first college game. Then she went out and lived up to her billing.

Cheryl was one of the few players in the history of women's basketball who could play all five positions. At 6-foot-2 she had enough size to play the post or the wings. She also handled the ball well enough to play point guard. She had the range to play shooting guard.

Cheryl, who came out of Riverside, California—and whose younger brother Reggie is the star of the Indiana Pacers—wasn't the only outstanding freshman Linda Sharp had recruited for the 1982–83 season. From the Bronx Coach Sharp brought in a true point guard named Rhonda Windham.

Rhonda had been a two-time New York City Player of the Year, which meant she had serious game. She was 5-foot-5, quick as lightning and could jump out of the gym. She was real savvy about reading the court and getting the ball to the right people. On defense, she was feisty and aggressive.

Rhonda came in as a true freshman and ran the show. Even though she had to deal with all the different personalities and egos out on the floor, she decided what was what. When Rhonda said she wasn't going to give you the ball, there was no point in arguing your case—you weren't getting it. If Rhonda said "Wait until next time," that's exactly what she meant.

She was a real floor leader. She had to be strong-willed to be the point guard on that team—and she was. Rhonda showed up at USC and took over, just like that. That's not easy for a freshman to do.

Between the McGee sisters and Cheryl Miller in the front-court, and Rhonda Windham at the point guard, four of the Lady Trojan starters were set. The 1982–83 season began with Kathy Doyle, a 5-foot-10 senior, as the fifth starter. That relegated me to the role of sixth man—the first player off the bench.

Coach Sharp tried to encourage me by saying I would be a "super-sub" or "spark plug" off the bench, but I took the news that I wasn't starting as a slap in the face. I thought Coach

Sharp was dogging me, not letting me become the player I could be.

I was unhappy with the situation. I felt I was good enough to be a starter, even a star. I let everyone around me know it, too. I carried myself with a confidence that bordered on cockiness.

When I didn't make the starting lineup, I pouted briefly and then went to see Coach Sharp to find out why. Whatever reason she gave wasn't good enough for me, but I didn't complain. I was a good soldier.

Kathy Doyle, though, suffered a serious knee injury early in the 1982–83 season, and I took over her spot as a starter at off-guard after seven games. Yolanda Fletcher, a sophomore, and Juliette (JR) Robinson, a junior, also got some extended minutes in the Lady Trojans backcourt. But mostly it was me and Rhonda Windham in the starting backcourt, with Rhonda bugging me by not giving me the ball to shoot.

What can I say about my sophomore year? It was Cheryl Miller's show and everyone knew it. Our role was to pass the ball inside to Cheryl or the McGee twins. Occasionally, defenses packed down so tightly that I was called upon to loosen things up with some outside shooting. Most of the time, though, we all just worked the ball down low.

The Lady Trojans that year averaged almost 86 points a game and broke 100 points five separate times. We got almost 60 points a game (58.0) from the "Big Three." Cheryl averaged 20.4 points. Paula and Pam chipped in with 19.2 and 18.4 apiece. I'd have to admit that Coach Sharp's offensive strategy worked extremely well, even if it did shove me into the background.

I realize now it wasn't my time to shine or be individually rewarded. I think both my sophomore and junior seasons at USC were tests the Lord had me go through to see if I was going to be a selfish player. He must have wanted to see if it was going to be a case of I-I-I or whether I would be putting my team first. The test was to see if I would ruin the chemistry of the Lady Trojans.

I didn't.

Yes, I wanted to be given the burden of scoring 25 points a game or hitting the winning jump at the end of the game. I could have handled that, no problem.

But that wasn't my role on the Lady Trojans, so I sacrificed my own game. I didn't do it willingly, or happily, but I made sacrifices for the team because I realized they were necessary for us to win a championship. That was my ultimate goal at USC, playing on a championship team. Fortunately, I was rewarded.

Twice.

The 1982–83 Lady Trojans started the season with a 13-game winning streak, including impressive road wins over powerhouses Louisiana Tech and Tennessee. Then we lost two consecutive games. Louisiana Tech beat us 58–56 in a rematch in Los Angeles, and our main WCAA rival, Cal State Long Beach, nipped us 74–73.

That was it for the losses. We reeled off 18 consecutive wins, all the way through the NCAA playoffs. As our winning streak grew, crowds at the Sports Arena began picking up. Instead of playing before 1,000 fans or less, as we had during my freshman year, we started drawing crowds of 2,000 and more.

The student body was getting excited, and even a few of the Hollywood stars, like Tom Selleck, came out to see what was going on. On the road, we consistently set attendance records, which was because of our high national ranking and all the publicity Cheryl Miller and the McGees were receiving.

We won the NCAA West Regional championship by beating our WCAA conference rival, Cal State Long Beach, 81–74. The 49ers were a tough team. They still had LaTaunya Pollard, who with a 30-point average led the WCAA in scoring, and a real good point guard named Faye Paige. Pollard scored 37 points against us in the regional finals, but we had too many weapons for them.

The NCAA women's basketball championship in 1983 was played in Norfolk, Virginia, with Old Dominion University—which had won two national titles in the late 1970s during the heyday of Nancy Lieberman—serving as the host.

Our opponent in the semifinals was Georgia, which had an outstanding young guard named Teresa Edwards, one of the best talents women's basketball has ever produced. But Georgia didn't have the size to match up with our inside game, and we routed the Lady Bulldogs 81–57.

That win put us in the finals against defending national champions Louisiana Tech, which had defeated Old Dominion 74–60 in the other semifinal. We had already split two games that season with the Lady Techsters.

Louisiana Tech had some real good talent in its lineup, including Debra Rodman (who has a rather well-known brother), Janice Lawrence and Pam Gant. At point guard was Kim Mulkey, a quick and intelligent floor leader.

We got off to a real slow start in the championship game and trailed by 11 points at the half. We were outshot, outrebounded and outhustled.

But Coach Sharp lit a fire under us at halftime, and we used a pressure defense to force some turnovers and get the momentum turned around. We surprised the Lady Techsters with a full-court press that we'd been working on in practice since January but had never used in a game.

We kept cutting into Louisiana Tech's lead until finally, in the closing minute of play, Paula McGee hit a short turnaround shot in the lane that broke a 67–67 tie.

USC regained possession in the waning seconds, but Tech's Kim Mulkey tipped the ball away from Kathy Doyle, who had replaced Rhonda Windham at guard when Rhonda fouled out, and started a two-on-one fast break. I raced back on defense and as soon as Mulkey passed to Debra Rodman, I stepped in front of Kim and took a charge. That was a bit ironic because no one in America took more charges than Kim Mulkey.

Louisiana Tech had no choice but to foul. Cheryl Miller missed the front end of a 1-and-1 with six seconds to play, but we hounded Mulkey so tightly Kim was unable to get off a shot before the buzzer sounded. The Women of Troy were national champions.

When I came to USC, I had been mostly an offensive-minded player. Coach Sharp thought I was a little too one-dimensional, and she made me work hard on improving my defense. At the most critical moment of the season, I had stepped up and made the key defensive play. Who would have believed it?

We put it all on the line that day. I think Rhonda Windham said it best: "What made the comeback work was not so much athletic talent but heart. We really put our hearts on the line today."

In the interviews after the game, I gushed, "We expected to win. I knew we could do it. Nobody can stop us. I think a dynasty is forming." Even then, I was an excitable girl. My game was based on energy and emotion.

While we were winners on the court, I continued to struggle making adjustments to college life. Nothing came easy for me. I still had trouble making my grades and making friends. I still felt less than equal to the other students.

What cheered me up in those days were letters I received from Ricky, who had left home by then and was serving in the U.S. Army in Texas. Ricky wrote to me and told me to be strong and keep believing in myself. His words had a way of lifting my spirits when nothing else could. Just thinking about him wiped away the frowns.

The other positive thing in my life was that I had begun dating Mark Robins on a regular basis. But, like a fool, I believed Mark all the times he told me we couldn't go out because he had another commitment.

Those commitments turned out to be another girlfriend. At the time, I was too naive to know it.

My constant academic struggles caught up with me later that year. I was ruled academically ineligible during the fall semester of my junior season. I had to sit on the sidelines while my Lady Trojan teammates started the 1983–84 season, Cheryl Miller's second and the fourth and final for the McGees, without me.

Rhonda Windham was on the sidelines as well. Rhonda had severely injured her knee in the summer of 1983 while playing at the U.S. Sports Festival in Colorado Springs. She needed to have major reconstructive surgery and would be unable to play during the entire 1983–84 season.

I remember driving nine hours from Los Angeles to Lake Tahoe, Nevada, to be with Rhonda after her surgery. I hung around the hospital for several days with Rhonda and her mom, trying to cheer them up and lift their spirits. Rhonda was really down, but I knew she wouldn't stay that way. She's such a strong person that I knew she would come back tough. She did.

Linda Sharp had a tradition of hosting a Kris Kringle party for the Lady Trojans each year, either at her house or at Heritage Hall on campus. She gave out little gifts to the players, gifts that carried a message.

At her team party that Christmas, Coach Sharp handed me a dunce cap and a mortarboard. I'd never seen a mortarboard and didn't know what it was. Coach had to explain it to me. She said I was either going to make my grades and rejoin the team (in which case I deserved a mortarboard) or remain ineligible and be a dunce.

A few days later, my grades for the fall semester were posted. I was so excited by how well I'd done that I went running out on the court, interrupting practice, wearing the mortarboard and a big grin. My teammates greeted the news with a big cheer.

Coop was coming back.

The 1983–84 Lady Trojans won their first ten games of the season. Then we went on an extended road trip and lost consecutive games to Texas, Louisiana Tech and Old Dominion. None of those teams was a pushover, mind you. They were all top ten teams and legitimate candidates to take away our NCAA title.

With Rhonda Windham missing at point guard, Coach Sharp used a variety of players in the backcourt. Yolanda Fletcher and Juliette Robinson played long minutes at times. We also got a big contribution from Amy Alkek, a sophomore from Victoria, Texas. We missed Rhonda's brand of leadership on the floor, but the other guards stepped up their play in her absence.

Cheryl Miller averaged 22 points a game as a sophomore and again was named to every All-America team. The McGees, meanwhile, combined for nearly 32 points a game. Paula scored 14.7 points while Pam averaged 17.2 (outscoring her sister for the only time in their careers).

I again was the Lady Trojans' fourth leading scorer. I averaged 9.3 points as a junior—roughly the same as my sophomore year. My season high of 20 came in a WCAA conference game at Cal State Fullerton.

I vented a lot of my personal frustration that season to Fred Williams, a new assistant coach. Because Coach Williams had grown up in the inner city, too, I felt he could relate to me and my problems. I used him as a sounding board.

Coach Williams became a good friend, which he remains (he's now an assistant coach with the WNBA's Utah Starzz). He was several years older and more mature, and he was able to keep me on a straight path whenever I started to veer right or left.

I credit Coach Williams with helping me see that although I was a smaller piece of the championship puzzle than some of my teammates, the puzzle wasn't complete without me. Cheryl Miller and the McGee twins may have been bigger pieces in the puzzle, but the team needed my contribution to win another championship.

We tied for the WCAA conference championship with Cal State Long Beach, each posting a 13-1 record. We beat them at our place, and they beat us at theirs.

We faced the 49ers for a third time that season—in the finals of the NCAA West Regional. The game was at the Sports Arena, our home court. We used the energy from the crowd to race to a 91–73 win.

We were going back to the Final Four, and we didn't have to go far. The NCAA championships were set for Pauley Pavilion on the UCLA campus.

In the semifinals, we saw the familiar faces of Coach Leon Barmore and his Louisiana Tech Lady Techsters. We avenged the loss they had pinned on us early in the season, winning 62–57. Cheryl Miller led the way with 22 points.

I hurt my knee in that game during halftime. Cheryl came into the locker room steaming about some call—or noncall—and in her frustration, she kicked a trash can. The trash can accidentally hit me flush on the kneecap and left me hobbling around for a while.

Our opponents in the finals were the Lady Vols from Tennessee, Pat Summitt's team. Like Louisiana Tech, they had defeated us during the regular season.

But not this time. The McGee twins closed out their college careers with a great effort, each scoring 17 points to lead us to a 72–61 victory. We led almost all the way.

I suffered a hyperextended knee in the championship

game against Tennessee. I had just released a free throw when the girl boxing me out lost her balance and crashed into my knee. After a couple trips up and down the court, I knew something was wrong with it.

But there was no way I was going to come out of that game. At the next timeout, I told our trainer, Leah Putman, to tape it so the knee would stay in place.

The Women of Troy had repeated as national champions, joining a select group of schools—Immaculata (Pennsylvania), Delta State (Mississippi) and Old Dominion—that had won consecutive titles either in the NCAA or its predecessor, the AIAW. (Tennessee, as noted, has since joined the list.)

A few weeks later, my teammates and I received an invitation from the White House. President Ronald Reagan, a former governor of California, wanted to have a special reception for us.

I remember having to search for an outfit to wear. I finally found a white suit, with mid-calf pants. I wore white hose and white shoes. I thought I was pretty sharp.

Looking back, I realize now I didn't have the proper respect for the White House visit or an appreciation for how special we were to receive an invitation from a U.S. president.

And it was only after I'd been overseas for a few years and gained exposure to some of the European capitals that I understood what a historic and extraordinary city Washington is.

At the time, I didn't know anything about how to tour around and see new sights. There isn't much of a tourism business in Watts.

In those days, I went where I was told, when I was told. I really didn't know how to enjoy myself—unless I was playing ball.

Chapter Nine

The Darkest Days of My Life

The thrill of winning a second straight NCAA championship and getting to visit the White House with Coach Sharp and my teammates wore off quickly for me.

When the 1984 Olympic Games came to Los Angeles that summer, and the U.S. women's basketball team won the gold medal, I didn't share in the excitement. I couldn't afford a ticket to any of the games and no one invited me to watch my USC teammates Cheryl Miller and Pam McGee win gold.

I was out of the loop. I didn't feel a part of the USC family. Even though my coaches and teammates did everything in their power to make me feel like a member of the family, I felt like an outcast.

Pressures began to build up all around me. I saw my mother struggling trying to make ends meet. She seemed weary and worried, tired and tense. I could see those things in her face and hear them in her voice.

Ricky had come home from the army and was having troubles with too much drinking. He started showing some destructive behavior. He started being abusive to my mother, saying mean and hurtful things.

My oldest sisters, Joanne and Drena, had their own families by then and were out of the house. Stephanie, Lisa and I did our best to hang together and make things as easy on my mother as we could.

I began having difficulty again academically. As I said, I was always having to play catch-up at USC and now it seemed I had fallen further behind in my studies.

I was redshirted for academic reasons in the fall of 1984, at the start of what should have been my senior year. Not being able to play basketball, which was my burning desire, had a devastating effect on me.

I was crushed. I couldn't use basketball as a release for all the tension, frustration and anxiety I was feeling.

Besides all the other stuff bringing me down, my relationship with Mark had deteriorated. I found out he was involved with another woman, who was pregnant with his child. I probably should have been able to read some of the telltale signs, like the little snide remarks his friends made about me or how when I went to visit Mark at his home his mother would act like "What's *she* doing here?"

But my relationship with Mark had been my first experience with being in love, and I was innocent and naive. The expression "love is blind" must have been meant for me.

I needed some help solving my problems, but I felt too ashamed to ask for any. I finally made the decision that my family needed me more than the Lady Trojans did. I felt I was the only person who could provide a solution to the problems my mother was having at home—by getting a job and helping out with the family's finances—so I decided to drop out of school at the beginning of 1985.

It was a decision I made all on my own. I didn't tell anyone, not even Mother. I knew she would be disappointed in me.

I didn't tell Coach Sharp or Coach Williams what I was doing because I knew they would try to convince me to stay in school. I knew that hearing such talk would make me feel bad about my decision to leave, and that would add more pressure.

I had enough problems to deal with without having to feel guilty about leaving my coaches and my teammates.

I knew my USC coaches cared about me and would want to try to help me, but they didn't know about all the pressures building up at home in Watts, and I had no intention of telling them.

I went looking for work to help support my mother. I told myself that I wasn't going to flip hamburgers or sack groceries, either. I was going to get a job with a future, a job where I could excel.

I got hired as a teller at First Interstate Bank in Inglewood, a short drive from Watts. I went to work with the attitude that I may have been starting as a lowly teller, but I was going to wind up as the president of the bank.

No matter how many steps it would take to work my way up, that's what I was going to do. I was determined to be the best worker they had at that bank.

Coach Sharp tried contacting me several times over the next few months, but I didn't return her phone calls. There was nothing to say. She had a team to coach, and I had family matters to deal with.

I spent my days at the bank processing deposit slips, cashing payroll checks and doing all the routine banking duties that tellers do. To be honest, I liked being around all the money because I'd never seen much in my life. During the several months I worked there, I earned a promotion to head teller.

USC seemed far, far away. After two straight national titles, the Lady Trojans struggled during the 1984–85 season. Coach Sharp still had Cheryl Miller, and Rhonda Windham returned from her injury, but the team didn't come close to its previous level.

USC went 21-9 that year, 10-4 in the WCAA. Old rival Cal State Long Beach knocked USC out of the NCAA playoffs in the second round. But I was too busy with my own problems to pay attention to the team's success or failure.

I discovered after working for several months at the bank that my life was incomplete without basketball. I had to have it.

I missed the game so much that I started playing at night, after work and on the weekends. I played a lot of pickup games with a friend named Dwan Hurt. I met Dwan through his brother, who ran one of the summer leagues in Los Angeles.

I also played a lot of one-on-one, often at midnight at El Segundo Park, with Leland "Pookey" Wigington. We had met a couple years earlier at the North Gym on the USC campus. Pookey stood barely five feet, but he was sensational on the court. A true artist.

Pookey was a star for Morningside High in Los Angeles and went on to have an outstanding career at Ventura Junior College. Then he was recruited by Seton Hall and played on the P. J. Carlesimo team that reached the NCAA finals (losing to Michigan) in 1989. Pookey's now a successful entrepreneur in New Jersey and among his business interests are artists representation and sports management. He's one of my closest friends and most trusted advisors.

About the same time I rekindled my passion for basketball, the people at USC began reaching out to me. Linda Sharp drove down to Watts to pay me a visit, but she couldn't find the right house. When I heard about that, I called her and said, "Don't ever do that again!"

I was worried she could have been harmed.

Fred Williams came looking for me, too. Strangers weren't

welcome where I lived, and when the guys hanging around on the street corner saw him, they surrounded his car and demanded to know who he was and what kind of business he had down there.

Fred explained he was looking for me, that he was my coach at USC. He wasn't sure anyone was going to believe him, until one of the guys went up to our front door and asked if anyone inside would vouch for this stranger. One of my sisters did.

Early in the summer of 1985, while still working at the bank, I went with a tour team to Mexico arranged by Joe Bettencourt. Joe, who acted like an agent, or broker, had connections to professional teams in Europe (who paid him a finder's fee to recommend talent). Players on a tour team try to showcase their talents so they can land jobs overseas.

I showed enough game on that trip to Mexico—we played exhibition games in Mexico City and Puerto Vallarta—that after we got back to Los Angeles, Joe contacted me and said a team in Austria wanted to sign me.

I had come to a crossroads in my life: Should I keep my job at the bank, where I was making progress and decent money, or take the better money being offered by a professional team? Should I stay and help my family?

I decided the president of the bank didn't have to worry about me taking his job. I chose the great passion in my life, basketball. I began making plans to follow my hoop dreams to Vienna.

Before I left town, Fred Williams reached me by telephone and gave me his best sales pitch about coming back to USC. He insisted that I should finish my career with the Lady Trojans.

Coach Williams had talked over my academic standing with USC advisor Willie Wu. They figured out that if I enrolled in the second semester of summer school and passed enough hours, I would regain my eligibility for the fall.

I told Fred about the professional offer. The team in Austria had already sent me a plane ticket, and I was scheduled to fly from Los Angeles to Vienna the very next day. He said it didn't matter, that I should be thinking about USC instead of Europe.

I told Fred I would let him know something right away. Then I sat down and talked things over with my mother.

The whole time I had been working at First Interstate, my mother had been saying to me, "Go back to school, go back to school. Don't worry about me, I can work things out. I don't need your help. I can work more overtime hours. You get yourself back in school."

I had been ignoring her. I was being as hardheaded as I had been as a young schoolgirl.

This time, I listened to her. She didn't want me going away to play ball. She told me I should finish what I had started at USC.

My mother said stay and play, so I did. I reenrolled in USC the next week. A few days later, I had a meeting with Coach Sharp. I figured she would chew me out for having left the team, but she surprised me by being positive and supportive.

Coach Sharp told me finishing my education was one of the most important things I would ever do. She also told me that she knew I wasn't a quitter.

I don't think Coach Sharp even mentioned the time I'd been gone from the team. She was focused on the upcoming season, not the past one, and she knew what I could add to the team in talent and experience.

My senior year should have been one of the best years of my life, but it got off to the worst start imaginable. Ricky, my favorite playmate as a child and the person who, next to my mother, had inspired me the most, died on October 4, 1985.

Ricky had gotten into a fight with another man, and Ricky was stabbed. Stabbed bad.

I was home in Watts on the evening of October 3. We got a call late that night from a friend of Ricky's, who said my brother had been seriously injured in a fight. He had no other details, like how bad Ricky was hurt or where he'd been taken.

I didn't know what we could do other than wait for the police to call or come by, so I told my brothers and sisters to go to bed and to say a prayer for Ricky. We'd figure something out in the morning.

When my mother came home from work around 6 A.M., Chucky went in and told her the terrible news. Mother started calling around to local hospitals and finally found out that Ricky had been taken to Martin Luther King. The people in the admissions office could tell her only that Ricky was listed in grave condition.

We rushed over to the hospital and learned that he was heading into surgery. I got to spend a few moments alone with him. I held Ricky's hand, kissed him and told him that I would love him forever. He died during the surgery.

Our whole family was crushed. We were lower than low. A bunch of people from our church, Rejoice In Jesus Ministries, came over to comfort my mother. I got in my car and drove straight to San Diego to be with my new boyfriend, Billy Washington.

I cried all the way down there, all the time I was there and all the way back. Billy and his mom did their best to comfort me. I remember going to a mall with Billy and just walking around holding hands. Neither of us knew what to say.

I drove back to Los Angeles the next day, and to take the burden off my mother, I became a rock. I shouldered the load for the funeral and burial arrangements. I made sure all the details were taken care of and that Ricky left this world with dignity.

I didn't let anyone see my grief. I had felt rejected and heartbroken when Mark and I split up, but the pain associated with losing my closest brother was a hundred times worse than that. A million times worse.

I was totally devastated. I ached all over. But I had to be strong for my mother and family, so I internalized the pain.

I suppose you could say that Ricky was a victim of his environment. He tried to escape, and he did manage to get out for a short while. But in the end he fell into the same trap that has cost so many African-American men so dearly and tragically.

Chapter Ten

No Longer
the Outcast

I kept my anger about losing Ricky bottled up inside for a couple of weeks, but one afternoon during fall practice I snapped. I was negative and disruptive. I argued with my teammates and got in their faces. All my pent-up emotions and feelings came pouring out in a tirade.

After my brother's death, for the first time in my life, I felt miserable playing basketball. I began to second-guess everything, including my decision to return to USC. With Ricky gone, I felt my mother needed me at home to help keep our family from being overwhelmed, not only by bills but by grief. I questioned whether it was worthwhile to continue my comeback with the Lady Trojans.

Coach Sharp called me into her office for a private meeting later that same day. "Look, Coop," she said, "you've always used basketball as your outlet, your release. I know you're having problems coping with everything else that's going on right now, but don't ruin the one thing [basketball] that's always been there for you." Later on, I had a similar conversation with Coach Williams, who reinforced the idea that basketball could be the one facet of life to lift me out of my state of depression.

I later realized I had never really given myself a chance to mourn. I was letting the anger and aggression I felt about Ricky's death affect my attitude and disrupt my performance as a player. I needed to let go of the pain.

My coaches and teammates stood beside me and helped pull me through. Ricky's death also caused me to reexamine my faith and spirituality. I leaned heavily on the Lord during this time of sorrow because I felt a void in my life no one else could completely fill.

It was at this point I realized God is always there for people who believe. We can praise the Lord during good times and lean on him when times are bad. I leaned on him hard.

While expanding my spirituality, I became more focused on the court. I dedicated my senior season to the memory of my brother and played with a vengeance.

On paper, the Lady Trojans looked like serious contenders for another NCAA championship. We had Cheryl Miller coming back for her senior year, and she had already been named an All-America three times and collegiate Player of the Year twice. Rhonda Windham returned to run the show at point guard, and Holly Ford gave us experience at forward. Holly's brother, Don, had played in the NBA.

Coach Sharp had recruited two outstanding freshmen, 6-foot-3 post Cherie Nelson and 5-foot-8 guard Karon Howell. Then there was me, back at shooting guard after a sabbatical at First Interstate Bank. Overall, we appeared to have a good nucleus. We anticipated another great season.

The Lady Trojans got off to a 5-0 start, four of our wins by margins of 30 points or more. Then we went on the road for an early-season shootout with the University of Texas at Austin.

The Lady Longhorns had one of the elite women's basketball programs in the United States. They routinely packed more than 10,000 fans into the Frank Erwin Special Events Center, nicknamed, because of its circular design, the Super Drum.

I received a big reaction from the UT crowd when I came out in the pregame introductions waving my arms over my head and chanting "Coop, Coop, Coop." The crowd liked my energy and audacity. Such enthusiasm was normal for me that year. I did whatever I could to fire up my teammates. I used my emotion as a motivating tool, showing leadership and no fear.

The Lady Longhorns handed us our first loss, a convincing 94–78 defeat. Even though Cheryl Miller had 31 points and 9 rebounds, and I chipped in with 23 points, hitting 7 of 10 shots in the first half, we were no match for Texas on the backboards. With Annette Smith, Fran Harris and the rest of the Longhorns pounding the glass, Texas had a decisive 35–22 edge in rebounds.

We bounced back with five more wins, breaking 100 points twice, and then we got hammered on the road by Louisiana Tech. Our high-powered attack, which was averaging over 90 points a game, completely fizzled. We scored 53 points—a season low and 22 less than the Lady Techsters.

In January, we faced our traditional rival, Cal State Long Beach. I ran a 104-degree fever before the game and vomited profusely, but there was no way I was going to miss that game. No way. I thought the team needed me, and I didn't want my teammates to feel I would ever give up on them.

I didn't add much to the Lady Trojans attack that night. I felt bad and played badly. We sustained our third loss of the season 76–75.

That 1985–86 season, for the first time, I began to receive some significant publicity. I guess people had written everything about Cheryl Miller that could possibly be written. Someone decided to go after new material.

In February, the *Los Angeles Times* wrote a long feature article with the headline "The Comeback Kid." The story touched on all the ups and downs during my career at USC and all the adversity I had to overcome. The reporter repeated one bit of Cooper family lore—about how I stepped into the streets of Watts during a gunfight and told the men to put down their guns and stop the violence. (To be honest, I have no recollection of that incident, but I've heard my mother and sisters tell the story so many times it must be true.)

In late March, before the regional round of the NCAA tournament, the *New York Times* wrote a profile under the headline "Getting a Chance after a Long Wait." I told the reporter about how Ricky always offered his support and how his letters, especially during my first two years at USC, helped me cope with the adjustment to college. My dizzy world stopped spinning when his letters arrived; they made me forget about my problems.

Before the NCAA championships began, we had finished runner-up in the Northern Lights Tournament in Anchorage, Alaska. We were upset 70–68 by Northeast Louisiana in the finals.

The Northeast coach paid me a huge compliment that night, using a box-and-one defense (where one defender shadowed me while the other four defenders played a zone) to try to slow me down. Cheryl Miller was out with a hand injury, and he must have felt I was USC's only remaining weapon.

I loved the extra attention and didn't mind the extra work of having to fight through double teams to get the ball. A defense designed specifically to stop me showed how much respect people had for my game.

I knew by then opposing coaches were mentioning me in their pregame talks; teams had to deal with Cooper as well as Miller.

The Lady Trojans got on a roll in the NCAA playoffs. We beat Montana in the first round and moved on to the West Regional at Long Beach, where we dispatched North Carolina 84–70.

That win set up a rematch with Louisiana Tech, which had whipped us so thoroughly earlier in the year. We turned the tables on the Lady Techsters 80–64.

USC was on its way to a third Final Four appearance in four years. We were no better than the second choice, though, because the University of Texas had extended its perfect record to 32-0 and was ranked number one. The other two Final Four participants were teams from the Southeast, Tennessee and Western Kentucky.

We breezed through the semifinals against the Lady Vols 84–59, led by Cheryl's 17 and Cherie Nelson's 16. I added 11.

We had played Tennessee early in the season at the Sports Arena, and it had been a tough, physical game. Cheryl exchanged elbows with a Tennessee post player and had been ejected from the game. In her absence, I stepped up and scored 24 points to pace our 85–77 victory.

This time, though, we jumped on Tennessee early with a full-court press and created turnovers that sparked our offense. Rhonda Windham shut down Shelley Sexton, one of the Vols' top scorers. It added up to a total team victory.

That set up a final game against Texas, which had blasted Western Kentucky 90–65 in the other semifinal. It looked like a great matchup of two explosive, high-energy teams.

At the press conference before the finals, Texas guard Kamie Ethridge noted how women collegians played the game for love, not money. "We grow up with the fact there is no pro league," she said. "We know we aren't going to be millionaires."

Texas jumped to an early lead behind the shooting of Fran Harris, and we spent a good portion of the first half trying to catch up. As soon as we did, Texas went on another run. The Lady Longhorns led at halftime 45–35.

Our chances for a comeback dimmed when Cheryl got into

foul trouble in the second half. She subsequently fouled out with 7:30 left to play. Texas had held Miller scoreless in the second half.

By then Cheryl had been named to her fourth consecutive All-America team, joining Ann Meyers of UCLA and Lynette Woodard of Kansas as the only players to accomplish that feat. Understandably, she was disappointed to have had her worst game of the season in the last game at USC.

I have to say this about Cheryl: The thing I respected most about her game was that she played with intensity. She hustled and worked hard. Sometimes players with that kind of talent don't put out maximum effort, but Cheryl did.

I shot 11-for-22 from the field and finished with a season-high 27 points. (For the season, I averaged 17.2 points a game, second to Cheryl's 25.4.) It wasn't enough. The Lady Longhorns again beat us decisively on the boards (42–32).

Texas freshman Clarissa Davis, who came off the bench as the sixth man, was the dominant player on the court, with 24 points and 14 rebounds. That performance followed her 32 points and 18 rebounds against Western Kentucky. Clarissa was named MVP of the NCAA tournament, joining Janice Lawrence (1982) and Cheryl Miller (1983) as freshman MVP.

Another player off the UT bench, senior Cara Priddy, scored 15 points. In the most telling statistic of the game, the UT bench outscored the USC bench 58–4.

Texas coach Jody Conradt later called her team the best in the history of women's college basketball. (Personally, I would like to have seen them try to beat our 1983–84 USC team.)

I took the loss to Texas in stride. "I played well and I played hard," I told the media. "This is my last game and I feel bad we lost. But this is not the end of the world."

Seven months earlier I might not have felt the same way. I might have thought the NCAA title game was the most important thing in life. But I had grown up a great deal during the

1985–86 season. And I knew the loss of a basketball game—even one for the NCAA championship—means nothing compared with the loss of your closest brother.

Toward the end of the spring semester in 1986, I was picked to represent women's basketball at the annual USC All-Sports banquet. It was quite an honor and made me feel important.

It was also the first time I had ever done any public speaking. I was nervous. Very, very nervous. Thank goodness I had a script to work from.

By the end of the evening, I felt I had taken a big step toward self-confidence and self-respect. When I tried to make some funny and clever ad libs, people had actually laughed. Their laughter and applause made me think that I did have some intelligence and personality after all.

The reception I received that night made me feel, perhaps for the first time, like a real part of the Trojan family. I was no longer the outcast.

Chapter Eleven

Seeking Confirmation

I believed that I was one of the best players in the United States by the end of my senior year at USC—on the same level with Cheryl Miller, Clarissa Davis, Teresa Edwards, Kamie Ethridge, Katrina McClain and the rest of the collegiate stars.

I just needed someone to second my emotion.

I didn't have as many credits next to my name as some players. I had been named All–Pac West in 1985–86 but to none of the All-America teams.

Being overshadowed didn't discourage me, however. I was used to that. All it did was fuel the fire burning inside me. I knew that even if I couldn't match résumés with some of the top U.S. players, they couldn't match my intensity and desire.

I immediately went seeking confirmation that my game was as good as I thought. The odyssey began in the summer of 1986 at Colorado Springs, where USA Basketball conducted tryouts for the women's national team. The team would be going to the Soviet Union to compete in both the Goodwill Games and World Championships.

My lack of status in the basketball world at that time was reflected by the fact that I was among 300 players who had to apply to take part in the first phase of the tryouts. I paid my own travel expenses to Colorado to take a shot at glory.

I was one of roughly sixty players selected from the original 300 to advance to a second phase of workouts. We were joined by about thirty invited athletes. These invited players included most of the big names in U.S. women's basketball. Many of them, like 6-foot-8 center Anne Donovan, had played in the 1984 Olympic Games or had other international experience.

Everyone assumed the players chosen for the U.S. national team would come from the group of invited athletes. I was determined to prove them wrong.

Among the group of thirty players invited to Colorado Springs by USA Basketball was a family friend from Watts, Doreatha Conwell. Doreatha, who was three years behind me in school, had also played ball at Locke High. She was 6-foot-2 and really quick. She had started her career at Locke the same year I started at USC.

Doreatha and I had played a lot of pickup ball together in Los Angeles, but we always wanted to be teammates. We had hopes she could join me at USC, but she didn't qualify academically. She spent 1985–86 playing in Texas, where she became one of the top junior college players in America.

Doreatha and I went to Colorado Springs—she as an invited athlete, me as a long shot who had to pay her own way—sharing a goal of playing together on the U.S. national team.

The ninety of us went through strenuous training sessions in Colorado Springs, doing offensive drills, defensive drills, shooting drills and three-on-two drills (known as the eleven-man drill) that demonstrate reaction time and decision-making. We broke into squads and played scrimmage games. We had three workouts daily—two during the day and one at night.

After three or four days, the ninety players were narrowed down to fifteen or twenty. My name remained on the list, but Doreatha, sad to say, didn't make the cut. She was having some trouble with one of her knees, which had been operated on a year earlier.

The remaining players then went through a minicamp for several more days before the roster was trimmed to the twelve players who would make up the U.S. national team. When the selection committee released the final list, in alphabetical order, my name was near the top—the only player from the original 300 to have survived.

Wow! Was I blown away. It was an awesome feeling to have beaten such long odds at the tryout camp. My selection to the U.S. team was the kind of confirmation I'd been seeking that I actually was a talented basketball player. I couldn't call home fast enough to give my mother the good news.

The U.S. team, led by coach Kay Yow, traveled to Moscow for the Goodwill Games and then went to Vilnius, in Lithuania, for the preliminary rounds of the 1986 World Championships. By then I wasn't as unsophisticated as I'd been on my first trip abroad—to the Jones Cup in Taiwan. This time, I didn't stay in my room or refuse to eat the food. I got out, moved around and soaked up the experience.

I did feel a bit overwhelmed in Moscow. Everything, like Red Square, for example, seemed on such a large scale. I had never seen so many huge buildings. One apartment building looked like a fortress, the wall surrounding it easily covering a full city block.

Overall, Moscow had a dreary feel. The taxis were dirty and cramped, and it felt like we were riding around in a little box. The hotel rooms were spartan and had only the bare necessities, like hot water. The beds were hard and the walls were unadorned. Luxurious they weren't.

Moscow wasn't like the European cities that I would travel to in later years, places where people are full of life and full of hope. Russian people, at least the ones we encountered, were cold and somber, their faces tight and drawn. Many of them had to stand in long lines for bread and other food items, which probably explained their attitude and demeanor.

No one in Moscow seemed happy. The people didn't laugh or smile. They weren't outwardly friendly either. It wasn't that they were rude to foreigners, or hostile, but they definitely were standoffish. They didn't roll out the welcome wagon.

I recall seeing one woman break into a big smile and being surprised that she had a mouthful of gold caps. After that, I noticed several other Russians had gold in their teeth. Maybe it was a status symbol.

One vivid memory was the way people on the street in Moscow would line up to drink beer from dispensing machines. What astonished me was that everyone drank from the same glass. People put coins in a machine (like one of our soft drink vending machines) and set a tall glass down under a spigot. They'd drink the beer, then hand the glass to the next person—who would put in a coin, set the glass down and repeat the process. Amazing.

I saw those beer machines all over the city, but I never saw more than one glass at any machine. And I never saw anyone wipe off the glass before drinking out of it. That threw me for a loop.

The atmosphere in Vilnius was a lot different from what I'd encountered in Moscow. People were warmer and friendlier and more interested in communicating (mostly through interpreters) with the foreign athletes.

Fans at the games in Vilnius—we played the preliminary games for the world championship there before returning to

Moscow for the semifinals and finals—were more animated and more into the action. All the energy in Vilnius helped make up for the lifelessness in Moscow.

What made the two tournaments in the Soviet Union that summer so special and intense was the battle for international supremacy in women's basketball. The United States and the Soviet Union hadn't faced each other in years.

America had boycotted the 1980 Olympics in Moscow; the Soviet Union had responded by boycotting the 1984 Olympics in Los Angeles. The Soviet Union had won gold in 1980 with the Americans absent; America had won gold in 1984 with the Soviets absent.

Which was the better team? Everyone in the sport wanted to know. The teams had been like two heavyweight boxers avoiding a title fight. When the big test finally came, it was scheduled on the Soviets' home court. In the eyes of many who followed women's basketball, that fact alone made America the underdog.

The U.S. national team nevertheless came through in grand style for Coach Yow, winning gold at both the Goodwill Games and the World Championships. One of the highlights was watching Anne Donovan block a shot by the Soviet Union's 7-foot-2 center, Iuliana Semenova.

Among the standouts for the U.S. team were Donovan, Andrea Lloyd, Teresa Edwards, Katrina McClain, Kamie Ethridge and Suzie McConnell, our captain. I played a minor role in the team's success. In one of the games against the Soviet Union, I provided a spark off the bench, turning a couple of steals into quick scores. Mostly, though, I sat and watched others get the minutes.

Just making the U.S. national team had confirmed that I could compete with the best players in the world and fed my belief that my time to shine was coming.

When I returned from Moscow, I had no immediate plans.

Because I still lacked several hours toward a degree, my returning to USC for the fall semester was one option. I had also heard about a women's professional league trying to get started in Los Angeles (several pro leagues had operated in the U.S. in the late 1970s and early 1980s, with sporadic and varying success) and decided to focus on that opportunity.

I went over to Burbank—home of the NBC studios and butt of Johnny Carson jokes—and took part in a tryout camp. In one of the scrimmages, I suffered a broken jaw. While playing defense, I had moved across the lane from the weak side to offer help, but I left my feet when the shooter made a pump fake.

As I jumped, she bent over. As I came down, I felt my legs fall out from under me. I landed squarely on my face, breaking the zygomatic arch (where the cheek meets the top of the jawline), a bone I'd never heard of.

I underwent surgery at Centinela Hospital in Los Angeles to repair the damage, and I still have a scar in my scalp as a reminder. The injury set me back briefly. I ate my meals through a straw for three weeks while my jaw healed.

By then, the 1986–87 professional season was gearing up in Europe. I called Bruce Levy, a sports agent based in New York, and asked him about my chances of hooking up with a team overseas.

Bruce basically said that teams in Europe were looking for frontcourt players (centers, forwards), not guards. He said about the only guard European teams had a serious interest in was Teresa Edwards, one of the U.S. national team stars.

Fine, I thought, my talents have been overlooked before. I'll make other plans. Before I could figure out what those plans might include, I heard from Joe Bettencourt, who had arranged the tour team in Mexico I'd played on in 1985.

The timing of Joe's phone call couldn't have been better. He said a team in Valencia, Spain, was desperately seeking an

American import. The Valencia team had a battle on its hands trying to stay in the first division of the Spanish League. Could I help out?

Joe said the one-year contract called for $18,000 plus benefits (an apartment and car). Not only was that $18,000 more than I was making at the time, I knew the job in Spain represented a beginning. It would give me a chance to showcase my basketball skills and possibly open some new doors.

I couldn't say yes—or *sí*—fast enough. I hung up the telephone and started packing my bags for Spain.

I was on my way as a basketball professional.

Chapter Twelve

A Brief Reign in Spain

Waiting to meet me at the airport in Valencia were representatives of my new employer, Samoa Betera. The Samoa Betera team took its name from the Samoa Club, a popular bingo parlor in Valencia that provided the team owner's principal income, and the fact that the club was based in Betera, one of Valencia's suburbs.

They got me settled into a furnished two-bedroom apartment in Betera, which I shared with La Koy Wooton, the other American on the team (league rules limited teams to two non-Spanish players on the roster). La Koy was a twin; between the James and McGee twins at USC and now La Koy in Spain, I seemed to run into more than my share of twins in those days.

In addition to the apartment, La Koy and I shared a two-door sports car with a hideous bright orange paint job and a manual transmission. I had limited experience driving stick-shift cars, but I was able to get around in Spain without incident. One of my favorite destinations was the McDonald's restaurant in Valencia, about fifteen minutes away. I lived off McDonald's hamburgers and french fries until I began to summon up enough courage to try the local cuisine.

I quickly discovered one Spanish specialty: paella. Paella is a rice-based dish usually made with either seafood or chicken. Seasonings give paella a yellow color. It's delicious.

Where we have barbecue and chili festivals in Texas, and people in Louisiana have gumbo and crawfish festivals, Spaniards have paella festivals. People would walk around in the plazas sampling various dishes made by cooks from different neighborhoods. Prizes were awarded for the best paella recipes and the competition was spirited. Bragging rights were on the line.

I really enjoyed mixing and mingling with all the people in the streets in Spain. There was no violence, no fighting, just flat-out fun. It was a pleasant change of pace from some of my experiences in the inner city, where when a crowd gathered it generally meant something bad had gone down or was about to.

From the beginning, I had a warm feeling about my new home. Valencia, the third largest city in Spain, sits on the eastern coast, near where the Balearic and Mediterranean Seas intersect. I liked to drive up and down the coastline, watching ships coming in and out of port.

The climate is sunny and warm, somewhat similar to that of Los Angeles. People in Valencia and Betera were warm and friendly and made everyone, including Americans, feel welcome. They were hardworking, down-to-earth people who knew how to enjoy themselves.

I've never been the kind of person who likes to go clubbing. I'm not a night owl, either. Friends know never to call me late at night because chances are I've gone to bed.

One thing I found out in Valencia, though, is that Spaniards don't start their partying until late. Really late. I mean, like two in the morning late. At that time of night, I'm hibernating. I can hardly function at all.

One night, I agreed to go to a club with several of my new teammates. I didn't really believe parties started as late as everyone said, so I insisted that we go at 1 A.M.

I found out that what I'd heard was right. This place was completely dead. By two o'clock, people finally started coming in and the pace picked up. By 2:30 A.M., even with music blaring throughout the club, I could barely keep my eyes open. By 3:30, I told the group I had to go home. I couldn't hang.

Meanwhile, the party was just warming up.

In the spring, Spaniards celebrate Carnival with a two-week festival of fun and games. One of the big events is to see which neighborhood can make the best float.

The people who made the floats proudly displayed them in the middle of a major intersection in their particular part of the city. They parked these floats in the middle of the street, forcing drivers to maneuver carefully so as not to damage their cars or the floats.

The floats were made with a plaster substance, the kind used for making a hard cast. It sort of reminded me of extra thick papier-mâché. The floats came in all shapes and sizes. Some neighborhoods made floats depicting cartoon characters like Mickey Mouse. I remember seeing one float that was a replica of the White House. Other floats featured famous figures in Spanish history that I didn't recognize. Maybe one of them was El Cid.

On the last night of the Carnival celebration, floats from each neighborhood were paraded down a major boulevard in Valencia. The scene probably resembled the annual Rose Bowl parade in Pasadena (something I'd never seen growing up).

Prizes were awarded for the best and most colorful floats. At the end of the judging, people started shooting off fireworks and all the floats were set on fire. That must have been for *buena fortuna*—good luck.

One of my Samoa Betera teammates, Gracia Romero, drove me around the city during Carnival so I could see all the various neighborhood floats. Gracia also introduced me to a lady who helped build the floats. That lady used plaster to build a small astronaut for me. She even painted the letters "NASA" on the space suit.

Gracia became my closest friend in Spain. She helped me learn to speak basic Spanish, and I helped her improve the English she'd already learned in school. In the summer of 1987, after our season in Spain was over, Gracia came to visit me in Los Angeles. I took her to Venice Beach and showed her some of the sights of L.A. We had a great time.

Because some of the Samoa Betera players held day jobs, our team practices were generally set for ten o'clock. That was pretty tough on someone like me, who seldom sees the other side of midnight. After practice, which generally ended around 11:30 P.M., some of my teammates would eat a large meal. Not me.

I was ready for bed.

But having that kind of workout schedule gave me plenty of time during the day to drive around, enjoying the sights and soaking up some Spanish culture.

I liked to go into all the food stores in Betera and Valencia. Unlike America, which has huge supermarkets for grocery shopping, Spain has a bunch of small specialty shops. There was a store for fruits. A store for meat. A store for fish. Another store for freshly baked bread.

I also spent a lot of time that season making the short drive from Betera to Valencia, visiting Gracia and her family. Gracia's mother, who worked, would come home for lunch each day and Gracia and her brother and sister would eat with her, beginning precisely at 1 P.M.

Everyone would have a leisurely meal, just talking and enjoying one another's company. There was none of the gulp-it-down-and-get-back-to-work mentality we have in America.

My European experiences—both in Spain with the Romeros and later in Italy—taught me a lot about creating a family atmosphere during meals.

In early 1987, my mother came to visit for two weeks and got to see a couple games. While I know she had a great time, I had wondered if she'd survive the experience. It was her first trip out of the United States and her first trip to Europe.

During Mother's visit, we had a rare cold snap. When she arrived, my apartment was freezing. Wow, was it ever cold! The heating unit in the apartment was a radiator fueled by propane. You hooked up a line from the bottle of propane to the radiator cap, opened a valve and—presto!—you had heat.

Only my propane bottle was empty, and I didn't know how to ask the landlord for a new bottle. I later found out that tenants were supposed to leave their empty bottles in the hall for a serviceman to refill. We got that worked out just before Mother froze to death.

She and I had a great visit, particularly because it was the first time in my life I had her undivided attention. None of my brothers or sisters was around to distract her; she was all mine.

My mother and I really began to bond during her visit to Spain. But I could tell that by the second week she had begun thinking about her responsibilities back in Los Angeles. One night she said, "I don't want to leave you. But I am ready to go home."

My mother knew I was safe and happy in Betera and that I'd made new friends like Gracia Romero. She could see I was busy growing and maturing and that pleased her very much. I knew she hated having me living on the other side of the world, but she realized that was necessary for me to pursue my dream.

My basketball skills, which were improving significantly,

didn't produce a dramatic turnaround in the number of victories for the Samoa Betera team in 1986–87. I was, however, able to help the club remain in the first division for 1987–88.

When I arrived in Spain, the team was at the bottom of the first-division standings. I don't believe they had won a single game. Over the course of the next several months, playing at home games or traveling by bus to Madrid, Barcelona, Mataró and other cities, we only won a handful of games. Four or five, as I recall.

We finished next to last in the Spanish League standings that season. The six worst teams then participated in a round-robin playoff to see which two would drop down to the second division for the following year. I got hot in the playoffs and led Samoa Betera to a win that clinched first-division status.

Despite Samoa Betera's poor record, I enjoyed a one-year reign as the leading scorer in the Spanish League. I became a scoring machine, pouring in an average of 45 points a game.

I was pumped. Not only was it my first professional experience, but it was the first time I had been a go-to player. I finally had my first real opportunity to showcase my talent. I was ready to shout—"Hey! Look at me. I'm on the scene."

I should probably point out that the level of competition in Spain wasn't as high as in the women's professional leagues in Italy, Israel, France and Greece. Players in Spain were somewhat mechanical in their movements and didn't possess a great deal of foot speed. I immediately discovered upon my arrival that I could use my quickness and speed to create layups or easy jump shots.

After that first season of pro ball, I received an offer to join the more highly regarded Italian League. Parma, whose officials I later found out had noticed me during the 1986 World Championships in Moscow, needed help in the backcourt. They really wanted to sign Teresa Edwards, but she had already made other plans. So they got in touch with Joe Bettencourt, who got in touch with me.

The Italians were offering a one-year contract for $35,000, almost twice what I earned in Valencia. I couldn't say *grazie* fast enough. The offer from Parma taught me an important lesson about always doing my best. When the Parma executives had gone to Moscow to watch Teresa Edwards play, they also noticed me. I learned that whatever you're doing, always give your best effort because you never know who's watching. You just never know.

Before I went to Italy, though, I played for the U.S. national team in the 1987 Pan American Games at Indianapolis. That experience, not an entirely pleasant one, put me back in the familiar role of underdog.

Chapter Thirteen

Dog Days
of Summer

I came back to the United States after my first season in Spain bursting with confidence. Averaging 45 points a game does wonders for a person's feelings about herself.

I joined up with the 1987 U.S. national team, scheduled to participate in the Pan American Games in Indianapolis. Many of the players were holdovers from the 1986 world championship team, and getting reacquainted with old friends like Fran Harris and Kamie Ethridge was a blast.

Kamie, in particular, had a big influence on me. She was active in the Fellowship of Christian Athletes (FCA) and got me involved. Kamie showed me by example how to deepen my relationship with my Lord and savior, Jesus Christ. She helped me grow and mature and focus on becoming the kind of person God wants me to be.

Coaching the U.S. team in the Pan Am Games that year was Jody Conradt of the University of Texas. I knew she was a great coach because she had led the Lady Longhorns to an undefeated season in 1985–86, when they beat us in the NCAA finals. The memories of that particular loss still lingered.

We trained in Austin at the UT facilities. We played intrasquad games and then scrimmaged against a military team from Fort Hood. We smoked 'em.

My jump shot was cooking that whole summer. I was lighting up everyone in practice. Killing them.

For some reason, though, Coach Conradt had a problem with me and my game. I don't know why, maybe she thought I was too cocky or had a bad attitude. Maybe she didn't like the more animated personality that had started coming out in Spain as my confidence level rose.

Whatever, Jody put me in her doghouse and wouldn't let me out. I had been performing as well as anyone on the Pan Am team—and everyone could see it—but Coach Conradt wouldn't give me a spot in the U.S. starting lineup.

I wasn't happy with the situation and let people know it. But I kept working hard in practice and kept filling the nets with jump shots. I must have voiced too much displeasure, though, because Jody called me in for a meeting one day and told me if I kept complaining she would send me home.

I bowed to her wishes and kept quiet. I couldn't afford to jeopardize my spot on the team. I knew that members of my mother's family were planning to drive down to Indianapolis from Chicago to watch me play.

Sure enough, when the Pan Am Games started, my relatives were in the house. Grandmother was there and so were aunts, uncles and cousins, some of whom I had never met. None of these people had ever seen me play in person.

Mostly what they got to see in Indianapolis was the back of my warm-up. Coach Conradt kept me glued to the bench. I was buried so deep in the rotation that when Kamie Ethridge injured her knee at the beginning of the Pan Am Games, the coaching staff called up Alisha Scott (who's now a Houston

Comets assistant coach, incidentally) from a second U.S. national team and played her at guard ahead of me.

I was fuming on the bench but didn't voice any displeasure. I kept my mouth closed and went along with the program. I told myself, though, that I wasn't going to let the situation shake my confidence. I vowed that when I finally got an opportunity to play, I was going to take advantage of it.

I knew that if I got in a game and played terribly, Coach Conradt would look like a genius for not using me. I wanted to prove to everyone that she was making a big mistake keeping me on the bench.

The opportunity I had been waiting for came up in the semifinal game against Cuba. The U.S. fell behind 11 points early in the game. Cuban defenders were laying back, giving us the outside shot. With that strategy, they were able to double-team Katrina McClain in the low post and cut off Teresa Edwards's drives to the hoop.

Desperate for some outside shooting and seeing the game slipping away, Jody finally sent me in. My sole focus at that moment was to hit some three-pointers and keep the Cuban defense from collapsing on the post. That would give Katrina more operating room and loosen things up for Teresa to penetrate.

I rocked the joint. I buried a couple of three-pointers and scored something like 11 points in five minutes. I spearheaded a rally that brought the U.S. team back from the double-digit deficit.

When I subbed out, I had to walk right by Coach Conradt, who hadn't said two words to me the whole time the team had been in Indianapolis. "I didn't take you out for any reason other than I thought you might be winded," she said. "I'm going to put you right back in."

I didn't care. I had accomplished my goals. I had given my

team a chance to win, and I had shown the members of my family that I had game. I was ecstatic.

As soon as I sat down, a little boy behind our bench started yelling at Coach Conradt, "Hey, put number 14 back in! Put number 14 back in!"

I loved hearing that. It made me feel super.

We finished off Cuba in the semifinal game and then beat Brazil, which had the great one-two tandem of Hortencia and Paola Da Silva, in the finals. We had won our Pan Am gold and I'd enjoyed another opportunity to visit with international athletes and learn about them and their cultures.

I didn't play much in the final game. Jody Conradt went back to her regular rotation, which didn't include me. But the scoring outburst against Cuba had made the whole playing experience worthwhile.

I had proven that Coach Conradt should have had me in her lineup all along. I was good to go.

Chapter Fourteen

Growing Wings in Italy

*L*ittle did I know when I went to Italy in the fall of 1987 that Parma would become my second home. Or that my experiences there over the next several years would help me evolve into a better basketball player and better human being.

I matured physically, emotionally and spiritually in Italy. You could say that I grew up. I learned to stop thinking about myself in terms of limitations or hardships or disadvantages and began to focus on areas of self-improvement.

I taught myself to speak fluent Italian and tried to absorb every aspect of the experience of living abroad. I began to travel whenever I had the chance, gaining a deep appreciation for Italy's art and history, its people and culture.

By the time I left Italy for good, after the 1996–97 season, I was intimately acquainted with the catacombs in Rome, the canals in Venice, the gardens in Florence, the lake in Como. I had been to the Leaning Tower of Pisa.

I remember on my first plane ride to Parma aboard TWA

the passenger seated next to me mentioned something about a fabulous cathedral in Milan. I nodded politely, like I understood him, but I had no idea what he was talking about. Eight years later, I could have discussed the architectural style and motif with him. In Italian.

The limited person I had been all my life—or assumed I always was—underwent a transformation in Italy. A renaissance, if you will. I changed from a lowly caterpillar into a specimen butterfly. I grew wings and flew.

Those changes occurred gradually. But the inner strength I began developing as a person and basketball player slowly fed on itself. The self-confidence I gained as an independent woman capable of making her own decisions made me a more assertive athlete, and my success as an athlete gave me more confidence as a woman.

When I first got to Parma, I lived on the top floor of a five-story residence complex owned by the team's owner, Gianni Bertolazzi. Five of my teammates lived on the same floor with me, and one, fellow American Alicia Jones, lived in a larger apartment on the floor below.

Those of us on the fifth floor had studio apartments with a kitchen, bathroom and living area. The apartments were maybe 400 or so square feet.

The residence complex was within walking distance of the Parma arena, the Palasport. Not that the weather was always conducive to walking. Because Parma is located in the north-central part of Italy—about an hour's drive south of Milan—the climate is colder and could be more severe than Valencia's.

And, because the Parma River bisects the city, a dense, thick fog often envelops the whole area, reducing visibility to a matter of yards or feet. Coming from Los Angeles, I'd seen a lot of smog but never fog.

Parma is an affluent city of more than 200,000. Many of its residents are involved in some phase of the food manufacturing and processing business. Not only is Parma the home of Parmesan cheese, but the city has a large plant for aging prosciutto (a type of ham). Tomato paste is another major food product produced in Parma. All the various food operations give the city an interesting aroma, though the predominant smell is of cheese.

All the jobs in the food business have raised the city's standard of living. When a boyfriend from back home, Alfonso Stubbs, came over to visit that first year in Parma, he looked around the city for a while and finally asked, "Cynthia, where are all the poor people?"

I'd never thought of it until then, but Alfonso was right. You never saw homeless people in Parma. You never ran into beggars asking for money.

The answer to Alfonso's question was, there weren't many poor in Parma. People there were fairly affluent. Many of them drove late-model sports cars, shopped in expensive boutiques and dined at gourmet restaurants. Many, like Gianni Bertolazzi and his family, lived in large villas.

I'd met Alfonso Stubbs in Los Angeles after my season in Spain. I saw him walking around in the Westwood area, near the UCLA campus, and went up and introduced myself. He was smart, handsome and funny—a great companion. We dated while I was home that summer, and he came to see me in Parma, but I knew I wasn't ready for a serious relationship.

Ricky's death was still too recent a memory and, deep down, I still had strong feelings for Mark Robins. Yes, I know, after all those years and after all he had put me through. I was still crazy about him. I talked about Mark so much that one day, in exasperation, Alfonso finally said, "Cynthia, why don't you just call him up and ask him to marry you?"

Alfonso and I still stay in touch. We can laugh about that story now.

The Parma team had a great coach, Antonio Morabito. He

was a terrific motivator, and he knew basketball inside and out. He loved the game. He ate it, slept it and never stopped talking about it.

We got along well, although we had to battle a constant communication gap. Coach Morabito didn't speak any English, and I had trouble (until I finally mastered the native tongue a couple years later) getting my exact point across to him.

I couldn't say what I meant in ten words or less, so I had to go the long way around, trying to make my point through a mishmash of English, Spanish and hand gestures. A lot of meaning either fell through the cracks or was missed entirely.

Morabito and I had a big misunderstanding one day that wound up with me getting kicked out of practice. As background, I should say that he had a habit of informing Parma's two American players (Italy had the same two-foreign-player limit as Spain) that he wanted us to be quiet by telling us to shut up.

"Shut up," he would shout, his voice rising for impact. "SHUT UP!"

Because I always asked questions about the plays we ran or the strategy behind everything we did, Morabito would frequently direct those two words at me.

I was certain he didn't realize there was a nicer, more polite way to tell the American players to quiet down and give him their undivided attention. So at dinner one night, I calmly explained to him—as best I could—that saying "shut up" to someone is rude and offensive.

At practice one day shortly thereafter, I started telling Morabito about the problems I was having with a particular offensive set we were working on. He grew impatient with me and finally screamed the magic words.

"Shut up?" I repeated. "Didn't I tell you that expression offends people?"

Morabito didn't want to hear another word from me. Slowly and emphatically, he said again: "SHUT! UP!"

I put one hand on my hip and dangled the other out in front of me, trying to give my best imitation of a lady. "Oh, you must mean like this," I purred. "Shuuuut uuuppp."

I guess he thought I was sassing him. He started waving his hands, chasing me off the court.

Even that was misunderstood. I thought he had kicked me out of practice. So I picked up my gym bag, left the Palasport and starting walking back to our residence complex.

I'd only gone a few blocks when here came the Parma owner, Gianni Bertolazzi, racing up on his motorcycle. "Come back to the gym," he said. "Morabito wants to see you."

"But he kicked me out," I protested.

"No he didn't," Gianni insisted.

I hopped on the back of his motorcycle and rode back to the Palasport. When I walked into the gym, Morabito stopped practice and waved me over.

"Who told you to leave?" he demanded.

"You did."

"I didn't mean leave the building," he said. "I just meant I wanted you to get off the court."

Oh.

Those kinds of gaps in communication occurred with most of my teammates, too. We had trouble, at times, getting on the same page. Adding degrees of separation on the team was the fact that a couple of the players became jealous when I arrived and took over as the team's leading player. In my defense, I can only say I was doing what I could to help our team win games. And I was doing it with Coach Morabito's blessing.

Parma got on a pretty good roll in 1987–88. We moved up from twelfth in the standings to fourth. We were a group of overachievers.

I became one of the dominant players in the Italian

League, scoring nearly 40 points a game (39.8). I was named both Rookie of the Year and Player of the Year. Those awards, which earned me small cash bonuses, were further confirmation of my growth as a player.

Even though the competition in Italy was more intense than in Spain, I had met the challenge. I had to beat out some of the world's best players, including Teresa Edwards and Janice Lawrence Braxton, to be recognized as the top player in Italy.

The awards fed my growing confidence as a basketball player.

I also made strides off the court. I began to teach myself to speak Italian and tried to use it in every conversation. I tried to immerse myself in the whole environment. I tried to think European and act European as much as I could.

When I was playing in Italy—and later Sicily—most of the Americans playing overseas never even bothered to try to adapt. They either hung out with other American players, or no one. They spent a big chunk of their paychecks calling back to the States to talk to their family. They didn't get out in the city much to meet new people or have new experiences.

I became friends with Gianni Bertolazzi, his wife, Cristina, and their children, Julia and Matteo. The kids were always hanging around at our practices, and I taught Julia and Matteo some fundamental basketball skills, like those Lucias Franklin once showed me. (Matteo, incidentally, now plays professional ball in Italy. I like to think I inspired him and helped him get off to a good start.)

Over the years in Parma, I began to think Italian and act Italian, using my hands to gesture when I spoke. Italy became such a familiar and comfortable environment for me that I'd face a bigger transition returning to Los Angeles at the end of one season than going back to Parma at the beginning of the next.

My family and friends were still living in Watts. Over time, it became harder for me to relate to the things they were going through. Spending seven or eight months overseas every year had expanded my horizons immensely.

I went home to America after the first season in Parma with one primary goal: earning a spot on the 1988 U.S. Olympic team. The Olympic Games were scheduled for Seoul, Korea, and I intended to help my country win a gold medal in women's basketball.

I already knew, from playing in the Goodwill Games and Pan Am Games and on the world championship team in 1986, that nothing gave me more satisfaction than playing for my country.

After a brief visit at home in Los Angeles, I flew to San Antonio to train with Eric Cooper. Eric had played college basketball at the University of Arizona before transferring to UT San Antonio.

Eric and I are like brother and sister (I refer to him as my "godbrother"). He helped fill the large void that Ricky's death two and a half years earlier had left in my life.

I met Eric when I was dating Mark Robins at USC. At the same time, Eric was dating Mark's niece, Marlo. Eric and I immediately became close friends. Whenever we were together, we played hoops.

Sometimes, we'd drive all the way down from Los Angeles to San Diego on Saturday or Sunday, playing pickup games of two-on-two. Other times, we'd just drive around Los Angeles checking out the action on the playgrounds. When we saw a bunch of guys shooting hoops, we'd get out of the car and call out, "We got next."

People were eager to give us a game because they viewed Eric as being at a disadvantage because he had a girl on his team. We never hustled any bets, but we could have made a fortune. We were hard to stop. Eric is 6-foot-4 and can sky; I had enough quickness to get my shot off on anybody. We wore people out.

After working out with Eric in San Antonio, I reported to the Olympic training camp in Colorado Springs in the best condition of my life. I had my Jheri curl juiced and my jump shot oiled. No one was going to stop this girl from getting on that plane to Seoul.

Chapter Fifteen

Heart and Seoul

After scoring 40 points a game in consecutive seasons in Spain and Italy, European fans of women's basketball might have reasonably expected me to emerge as one of the stars on the 1988 U.S. Olympic team.

I had shown an ability to assume the role of a team's leading player. Not only did I enjoy the pressure of having to solve a problem for my team, or hit the key basket in the closing seconds, I had demonstrated I was pretty good at being the go-to player.

Within the context of USA Basketball and the U.S. Olympic team, however, I was still viewed as less than—less than equal in ability to some of my teammates.

I had been busy proving myself overseas as one of the best players in the world, but people in my own country didn't regard me as anything special. I didn't have their respect.

My Olympic coaches did look to me to provide a spark off the bench with instant offense, or to change the tempo of the game with defensive pressure. But no one—except me—thought I should be in the starting lineup, much less the U.S. team's go-to player.

When the team America would send to Seoul was selected, there I was again: penciled in as the sixth or seventh player or eighth player, depending on the situation and the matchups we wanted on the court.

I set off for Seoul thinking that once again I'd be a minor piece in the championship puzzle. I swallowed my pride.

Under a United States Olympic Committee (USOC) program, athletes were allowed to take a spouse, family member or friend as a special guest. I invited my mother. I also used up a bunch of the frequent-flier miles I'd been accumulating going back and forth to Europe to buy an airline ticket for my sister Stephanie.

Mother and Stephanie stayed together in Seoul in a USOC-arranged housing complex. They came to visit me in the Olympic Village. Guests could only get as far as a certain point in the village; the interior was reserved for the athletes.

The best part of the Olympics experience for me was interacting with athletes from all different cultures. I learned from that experience that the key to communication isn't necessarily language but getting your point across, no matter how you do it. Some conversations transcend language. Smiles and laughter can go a long way.

I was hungry for knowledge about other people. I visited with athletes from Puerto Rico, Africa and Russia. I also hung out with members of the Italian Olympic team, some of whom were volleyball players living in Parma. (Parma had the best men's volleyball team in Italy in 1988, and several players had been named to the Italian Olympic team.)

In the Olympic Village, we had a huge video game room, a bowling alley and several rec rooms where athletes could hang out. My roommate for the Olympics was Teresa Weatherspoon (who now plays for the WNBA's New York Liberty). It seemed like Spoon and I were always paired up when the U.S. team traveled to international tournaments.

My teammates and I had a great time in Seoul. Because the U.S. Army has a large military installation there, security was real good. We weren't confined to the Olympic Village. We could go to the downtown area and do some shopping. I found a tailor who made custom sweatsuits and ordered several.

We also traveled to the army base in Seoul and loaded up on snacks and goodies at the exchange. A couple of times we went out to the base and scrimmaged against the men's team.

The American military personnel stationed in Korea were behind us all the way. They welcomed the U.S. Olympic athletes like family members. We knew we had their total support.

Another thing that made the experience in Korea so memorable was that U.S. coach Kay Yow actually gave me the opportunity to perform. She saw how well I was playing in practices and scrimmages and finally decided to adjust the starting lineup.

Coach Yow moved Teresa Edwards from shooting guard to small forward, replacing Andrea Lloyd, and put me in the starting lineup. I responded to my coach's vote of confidence by playing a major role as we swept through to the gold medal game, where we defeated Yugoslavia 77–70.

I averaged 14.2 points in the '88 Olympics, third highest on the U.S. team after Katrina McClain and Teresa Edwards, and played solid defense. Finally given a chance to do my thing, I excelled.

Right after the awards presentation, as the strains of the "Star-Spangled Banner" were fading away, I took off my gold medal and draped it around my mother's neck. I kissed her and hugged her and told her I loved her more than anything in the world.

The date was September 29, 1988. It was Mary Cobbs's fifty-second birthday.

How many mothers get to see their daughters compete in the Olympic Games? Not many. How many get to see their daughters actually win a gold medal? Even fewer. And how many mothers get to see their daughter win a gold medal on their own birthday?

The odds for something like that would be too high to calculate.

That day in Seoul still ranks as my single greatest thrill in basketball. Don't get me wrong: Playing on WNBA championship teams in the league's first two seasons has been fantastic. I love being with the Houston Comets. I love our city and our fans.

But my putting that gold medal around my mother's neck is a moment that can never be surpassed, much less equaled. Especially when you consider what both my mother and I had to endure to reach that special moment in Seoul.

With my sisters—(from left)
Joanne, Lisa and me.
Author's personal collection

I'm sitting on the left with
my sisters Stephanie
(middle) and Lisa (right)
on Christmas 1971.
Author's personal collection

At elementary
school with my
brother Ricky.
*Author's personal
collection*

Me at age eight.
Author's personal collection

All dressed up for my prom
at Alan Leroy Locke
High School in 1981.
Author's personal collection

Checking out some 1992 Olympics action with Julius "Dr. J" Erving and his wife.
Author's personal collection

With NBA legends—and Dream Team champs— Larry Bird and Patrick Ewing at the 1992 Olympics Dinner Ceremony.
Author's personal collection

With Earvin "Magic" Johnson, smiling as always, at the 1992 Olympics.
Author's personal collection

Posing alongside former Chicago
Bulls and Dream Team champion
Scottie Pippen during the
1992 Olympics.
Author's personal collection

Holding court with
"Sir" Charles Barkley at
the 1992 Olympics.
Author's personal collection

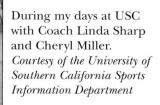

During my days at USC
with Coach Linda Sharp
and Cheryl Miller.
Courtesy of the University of
Southern California Sports
Information Department

With USC Assistant Coach Jean Agee during the 1983 NCAA championship. *Courtesy of the University of Southern California Sports Information Department*

Going up against Louisiana Tech's Pam Gant, a great shooter and one of my toughest competitors. *Courtesy of the University of Southern California Sports Information Department*

A shot of me at USC during the 1981–82 season. *Courtesy of the University of Southern California Sports Information Department*

With Parma team owner
Gianni Bertolazzi during the 1990
Ronchetti Cup championship in Italy.
Author's personal collection

With my friend Fran Harris at
the 1987 Pan American Games.
Author's personal collection

The 1992 United States Olympic Women's Basketball Team.
Photo by Steve Maikoski/Courtesy of USA Basketball

Playing in the Big Apple
against Vickie Johnson of
the New York Liberty.
*Photo by Manny Millan/Courtesy
of* Sports Illustrated

During a game against
the Phoenix Mercury.
*Photo by John W. McDonough/Courtesy
of* Sports Illustrated

Passing the ball with
the Houston Comets.
*Photo by Jim Gund/Courtesy
of* Sports Illustrated

The Comets offense getting
ready for a play.
*Photo by David Liam Kyle/Courtesy
of* Sports Illustrated

Putting up a shot.
*Photo by David Liam Kyle/Courtesy
of* Sports Illustrated

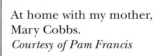

At home with my mother,
Mary Cobbs.
Courtesy of Pam Francis

Chapter Sixteen

Meeting My Idol

The highlight of my second season (1988–89) in Parma was having the chance to play against my idol, Lynette Woodard.

Lynette spent that season, and the previous one, playing for Priolo, an industrial city on the eastern coast of Sicily. It's no coincidence that Priolo won the Italian League championship in 1988–89. Lynette was talented enough to lead a team to a title. She could do it all.

I first heard about Lynette Woodard when I arrived at USC. She had been a four-time All-America selection at the University of Kansas, graduating in 1981. Lynette stands an even six feet and has a complete game. Drive to the hoop, hit the jumper, rebound with a fury, play tough defense—she's the prototype for the all-around female basketball player.

But more than a great ballplayer, Lynette Woodard is a class act. She always has a smile on her face and an encouraging word for everyone she meets. She's positive and upbeat. And she has a generous nature, giving back to her community and to the game of basketball. She's been a great ambassador for women's basketball and an inspiration to people who played with her or against her.

The first time Parma played Priolo, I was assigned to guard Lynette. She came out on the court all bubbly and bouncing, saying, "Hey, what's up, Coop? How you doing? Great job this season, keep it up." I could barely utter a word in reply.

The first time Lynette touched the ball, I was down in my defensive crouch thinking, "Wow, that's my idol. That's the real Lynette Woodard." She blew by me for a layup.

The second time down, she started to drive to the hoop. As soon as I started my backpedaling, she pulled up and drilled a jumper. The third time down, she grabbed an offensive rebound over me and put it back in.

It was as if my feet were frozen and wouldn't move. I had too much respect for Lynette, too much awe, to offer much in the way of resistance. She had her way with me. Used me.

At the half I had only scored something like 10 points, well below my average. We were trailing in the game, and my coach got all over me:

"Cooper, what are you doing out there?" he screamed. "Wake up!"

I snapped out of my daze in the second half and poured in 34 points, leading Parma to a comeback win. I wanted to show Lynette I had game, too.

The Parma team kept improving that season. I was more familiar with my teammates, and they were more familiar with me. Based on our improved standing in the Italian League, we participated in the Ronchetti Cup, a round-robin tournament between the top teams in Europe.

The Ronchetti Cup extends over several months and involves a great deal of travel. We played games in France, Spain, Austria, Greece, Yugoslavia and the Soviet Union, in front of loud, enthusiastic crowds. I soaked up as much culture as I could at each stop along the way. I stayed busy being a sponge.

The season ended on a bad note, however. I blew out my ankle in one of the final games. Eric Cooper had come over to visit that spring. It meant a great deal to me for any of my friends from America—but especially Eric—to see how basketball fans in Parma treated me like a celebrity, calling out my name and cheering my every move.

Eric was at the Palasport when I got hurt. We were playing Vicenza, the absolute best team in Italy at the time. I stole a ball and took off on a breakaway. Trying to chase me down was Janice Lawrence Braxton, who had been a college star at Louisiana Tech (we played against her in the '83 NCAA championship game) and a 1984 Olympian.

Right before I went up for the layup, Janice gave me a little hand check, which knocked me off balance. I came down with my weight on the outside of my left foot, not the middle. When that happened my left ankle rolled over and basically everything inside it—ligaments, tendons and the capsule that holds the ankle in place—snapped like the strings of a guitar. Man! I can still feel the pain.

Eric rode with me in the ambulance, and Gianni Bertolazzi met me at the hospital. A team of surgeons went in and did all the repair work they could.

I hobbled around for a good part of the summer. I wore a cast for about six weeks and then took another six weeks slowly working my way back into playing condition.

It took a while to clear the mental hurdle of going all out, without worrying whether my ankle would hold up. By that fall, however, the injury had healed and I was back at full strength.

Lynette Woodard had played on the U.S. Olympic team in 1984, along with my USC teammates Cheryl Miller and Pam

McGee. I remember seeing highlights of Lynette on television. She was as smooth as silk.

Lynette made history in 1985 by becoming the first woman to play for the world-famous Harlem Globetrotters. She received a lot of publicity when she joined the team, which helped raise the profile for all women athletes. She stayed with the Globetrotters for two years.

In the fall of 1989, officials with the Harlem Globetrotters contacted my mother in Los Angeles to see if I would be interested in becoming the team's designated female. I don't know exactly how that opportunity presented itself—if Lynette Woodard or anyone else recommended me for the job—but there it was.

My mother had grown tired, after two years, of me being away from home. She wanted me to come back and live in America, preferably near her. She wanted me to accept the offer.

I told Gianni Bertolazzi about the pending deal with the Harlem Globetrotters and indicated I'd probably be leaving Parma. Before I could say the words *arrivederci* or *ciao,* he offered me a huge raise to stay.

Bang! Just like that, out of the blue, he offered to double my $40,000 annual salary.

My momma didn't raise a fool. I immediately signed a new contract with Parma for the 1989–90 season, moved into a spacious one-bedroom apartment with a fireplace and continued my eight-month commute to Italy. (I did get to fly home, at the team's expense, each year for the Christmas holidays.)

My new apartment gave me privacy, which I'd never had living around my teammates in Gianni's residence complex. The apartment was located near downtown, where I liked to walk around and just be on my own. I went to theaters and watched Italian movies, which helped me pick up the language faster. I hung around coffee bars and outdoor cafes, soaking up the atmosphere.

The team had furnished me with a sports car, first a Renault and later a Fiat Y-10. But because so many people in Parma rode around on bicycles, I bought one, too.

That same 1989–90 season, I developed an interest in reading. I began to devour novels by authors like John Grisham, Robin Cook and Sidney Sheldon. I read the Agatha Christie mysteries with Hercule Poirot and Miss Marple. I also read the Bible and began listening to inspirational tapes my church in Los Angeles sent over.

I was already good friends with Gianni Bertolazzi's children, Julia and Matteo, but that season I became close to their mother, Cristina.

Cristina is a remarkable woman. She has a depth of knowledge about a great many subjects, like art, theater, opera, history and politics. She introduced me to the work of Wilbur Smith, who has written extensively about South Africa, and filled my mind with many new ideas.

With Cristina's encouragement and direction, I began making trips around Italy, mostly by train, to some of the major cities, places like Rome, Naples, Venice and Milan. Sometimes Cristina, who's probably ten years older, went with me. Sometimes I traveled alone.

By then I had enough grasp of the language to move around Italy comfortably and confidently. If I did get lost, I knew how to ask for directions and find my way home. Traveling by train is easy in Italy because the stations are generally close to the center of town. It's fast, convenient and not too expensive.

The experience with receiving an overture from the Harlem Globetrotters taught me a lot about my value as a basketball player. I had suddenly become one of the highest-paid players in Europe, and I realized, for the first time, my real worth.

I never looked at basketball as a business but as something I loved to do. When Parma paid me $40,000 a year I was amazed. When Gianni doubled my salary, I was speechless. But that was further confirmation that I was the kind of player I'd always dreamed of being.

After the 1989–90 season in Parma, where I again led the Italian League in scoring (33.0 average), I played on the U.S. national team at the 1990 World Championships in Kuala Lumpur and the 1990 Goodwill Games in Seattle.

Once again—I know this must sound like a broken record—I was placed in a supporting role by head coach Theresa Grentz and her assistant, Jim Foster. They used me as a spark plug, not a starter.

I particularly enjoyed working with Jim Foster, who's the head coach at Vanderbilt. He's a great people person. He's extremely knowledgeable about basketball, and he communicates well with his players. You feel his urgency and intensity, but you can also feel the trust he puts in his players. You know he wants what's best for you.

I've had a relationship of trust with several of my coaches—Linda Sharp, Kay Yow, Antonio Morabito and now Houston Comets coach Van Chancellor—and I know from experience that trust transmits to the court. You'll do anything for a coach who trusts you, and you'll always give your best effort.

I didn't feel bitter at the coaches' decision not to start me on the national team in 1990 as much as I felt disappointed. You might say it didn't matter anyway—because the United States won gold in both competitions—but it mattered to me. We beat Yugoslavia, which had the outstanding 6-foot-8 center Razija Mujanovic, in Kuala Lumpur. In Seattle, we beat the Soviets.

The best part of the trip for me was that Lynette Woodard was a member of those teams. By the end of the summer of 1990, my idol had become my friend.

Chapter Seventeen

Growing Pains

*B*efore leaving for Malaysia and the 1990 World Championships, I had reached a turning point in my life: I left Los Angeles.

I was tired of the hustle and bustle. Everything in L.A. seemed to be rush, rush, rush—and I just wanted to chill. I needed out of there, so one day I hopped in my car and took off for Texas.

I bought a home in San Antonio. I was familiar with the city from having trained there with Eric Cooper before the 1988 Olympic Games. Eric was still living in San Antonio in May 1990, and since he was my closest friend, that's where I went.

I contacted a local Realtor, who showed me some residential properties. I found a three-bedroom house with a fenced yard on the northwest side of the city. I immediately went shopping for furniture, kitchenware, towels, linen—all kinds of household items I'd never had to acquire before.

Leaving L.A. wasn't an easy decision to make, but I had to

move on with my life and I knew it. I needed a fresh start. I wanted to put some space between my present and my past.

I wasn't the same person anymore. I was no longer that little girl from Watts without any experience or vision. I'd been out in the world and seen ways to live other than my family's narrow existence in the inner city.

I no longer felt comfortable in a small, crowded house. I no longer felt comfortable in a dangerous neighborhood. Those things seemed normal when I was growing up in that environment. But now I knew they weren't normal at all. There were other—better—ways for people to live.

I had come to the realization that my experiences in Spain and Italy, adapting to different people and cultures, had put some distance between me and my family and friends. I felt a strong sense of separation. We had fewer things in common, fewer things to talk about. I had traveled to different countries while some of them had never been out of Los Angeles. They had no idea what even Torrance or Newport Beach looked like, much less Spain or Italy.

I was having trouble relating to their limited world, just as they had trouble relating to my expanded one. My expectations had grown beyond theirs.

I moved into a quiet, peaceful neighborhood in San Antonio. I jogged around the streets in the morning and evening. I joined a health club and enrolled in aerobics classes. I played basketball with Eric and his friends.

The pace was slow and relaxed. Maybe it had something to do with the heat. San Antonio—and all of South Texas, for that matter—can be blazing hot in the summer. You feel the heat, and at times you almost believe you can see it.

In San Antonio, I could kick back and relax. Sleep when I wanted to, eat when I wanted to—do my thing. I didn't have to worry about anybody's problems but my own.

I had plenty of time in San Antonio to reflect on family matters. I gained a deeper understanding of, and appreciation for, all the sacrifices my mother had made to keep us together.

Being away from Los Angeles allowed me to step outside the situation and gain a better perspective. I could see more clearly what my mother was going through, her needs and frustrations and everything that was happening.

When I was living in Los Angeles with her, it was hard for me to understand my mother's point of view at times. I had never been able to understand, for example, why she let my brother Kenny treat us the way he did, going off on us for no apparent reason.

When I stepped out of the situation by moving to San Antonio, I was able to realize, "Hey, he's her son, too. He's her blood. Her offspring."

I could see for the first time that she tolerated some of the things he did because in a way she felt at fault. She blamed herself because she couldn't give my brother some of the things he needed growing up or because there wasn't always a man around the house. And that's why she continues to try to help Kenny, even after some of us have lost our patience with him.

I returned to Parma for the 1990–91 season and once again led the Italian League in scoring. I broke through the 1,000-point barrier that year, totaling 1,015 points in 30 games, a 33.8 average.

By then I had reached celebrity status in Parma. Our games were broadcast live on the radio and were shown on TV, tape-delayed. It didn't hurt my image any with fans, or the media, that I could conduct postgame interviews in Italian.

People in Parma would stop me on the street or come up to me in the coffee bars and say hello or wish the team good luck. Fans would hang around after our games and ask me for autographs. I even started getting fan mail from Parma supporters. Not a flood, by any means, but a steady stream. I tried to answer as many letters as I could.

In Italy, like America, people want to associate with top athletes. All the attention I received was flattering, but because I was away from home, my feelings were bittersweet.

The official Italian League schedule consists of 30 games; the league has 16 teams and you play each of the 15 opponents twice, home and away. Games are played on Sunday afternoons, so the schedule takes 30 weeks to complete. High-ranked teams, though, may play as often as three times a week if they're competing in the Ronchetti Cup or European Cup or, in recent years, the Italian Cup.

As I mentioned, our team in Parma was improving each year. With more victories came more fans. In my first season, we probably averaged fewer than 800 fans a game. By the 1990–91 season, we must have averaged twice as many.

Fan interest continued to grow throughout the 1990s. By my final season in Parma, in 1996–97, we were one of the top teams in Europe and attracted crowds that probably averaged 2,000 or 3,000 a game.

I was slowed late in the 1990–91 season by a swollen appendix. I took anti-inflammatory medication to keep the appendix from bursting or rupturing. Once the season ended, I immediately underwent surgery and had it removed. I had plenty of time to go back to San Antonio and heal.

I was worried that the appendectomy could jeopardize my standing with the U.S. national team. It forced me to miss the Pan Am Games in the summer of 1991, and I was worried the coaches might want to keep the 1991 Pan Am team intact for the 1992 Olympics in Barcelona.

As it happened, though, the United States got upset in the Pan Am Games by Brazil. That loss told me that the coaches would probably want to fine-tune the U.S. roster for the 1992 Olympic team, which meant I was still in the picture.

I had another good season in Parma in 1991–92, finishing second in the league in scoring with a 26.5 average. For the first time in my career, I hit better than 60 percent from the field. Fifty percent is generally considered outstanding, especially for a guard.

But I had several disagreements with my new coach, Paolo Rossi. Friction surfaced between us, and he never would say what was wrong. He denied there was any tension, but I could feel it.

We went to a tournament in Brazil, and there was a mix-up about a morning practice. Everybody on the team knew the right time (10 A.M.) except me and Venus Lacy, the other American on Parma's team that year. She and I thought practice was scheduled for 11 A.M.

The players gathered in the hotel lobby shortly before ten o'clock. When someone asked where we were, Coach Rossi made a crack like "Let the Americans sleep, they must be tired." Everyone got on a bus and headed for the gym.

When Venus and I went down to the lobby an hour later, all we found was Gianni Bertolazzi. "Where's the team?" I asked.

"At practice."

I was furious. I never missed practice. I had been up that morning at 7 A.M., having breakfast and counting the hours until practice began. We hopped into a taxi and raced to the gym, where I confronted Coach Rossi.

"Why did you leave us at the hotel?" I demanded.

"I thought you were sleeping." He shrugged.

"Then why didn't you call our room?" I said. "You know I never miss practice."

I was really offended, but I let the matter drop. My teammates had started to gather around, and I didn't want to make a big scene.

From that point on, my relationship with Coach Rossi began to deteriorate. Over the next few years he began criticizing my game, saying that I was 50 percent the player I had been. He told me, to my face, that Parma should start looking for someone to replace me.

I didn't feel as though he was saying those things to motivate me. I believe he truly disliked me, though I never figured out why.

Another thing Coach Rossi did was make me run sprints before and after practice. I was already in top condition, but he said I had to do extra running. Looking back, I guess he may have been trying to force some kind of confrontation between us. Although it felt like I'd been singled out like that—I was the only player to whom the extra running applied—I did the extra work and didn't complain.

During both the 1990–91 and 1991–92 seasons, I continued to travel throughout Italy and expand my horizons. I knew that living overseas was a great opportunity—why waste it?

I visited beautiful cities like Florence, Siena and Livorno. I went to seaside cities on the Adriatic and Mediterranean coasts.

I played the tourist to the hilt. I bought a camera and shot rolls and rolls of film. I bought guidebooks and read up on the history and culture of every area I visited. I'd devour information on whether a city or region had a Roman influence, or Greek, or Arabic. I read about museums and architecture. I was hungry for knowledge and eager to grow as a person. I tried to absorb every last detail.

Florence definitely was my favorite escape. Venice, with its waterways, is different and unique. Rome has all that history. But Florence, in addition to its fabulous galleries and gardens, has a youthful spirit and ambience. There's a major university in the city, and the feeling in the streets and plaza is vital and electric. It also has great shopping.

I also deepened my friendship with Cristina, who continued to be my mentor and guide. She gained my total trust and confidence.

Cristina carries herself with elegance and class. She has

dark hair, brown eyes and an average build. She is a housewife, who stayed home taking care of Julia and Matteo while they were growing up. Some people think housewives are not intelligent, because they don't have their own careers, but Cristina is remarkably insightful.

She reads constantly. Books are her window to the world. When we went on trips together, she already knew everything about the places we were going.

Cristina and I became friends initially because she saw the effort I was making to learn the Italian language and the ways I was trying to fit into the culture. She got to know me first as a basketball player on her husband's team, but she was perceptive; she picked up on the fact that something was bothering me.

She looked beyond the wall I had erected around myself and saw a woman who was hurting. Cristina wanted to be friends with the person in pain, not the basketball star.

We began having long talks. We'd go to lunch at restaurants in Parma and talk for hours and hours. We bonded even more after I met her mother and her sisters and got acquainted with their families. After that, our conversations became more personal. We'd talk about problems and issues in our lives.

I'm not exactly sure why I unburdened myself to Cristina, but I did. Maybe it was because she was older, more mature and wiser in the ways of the world. Maybe it was because she was so warm, understanding and compassionate.

Or maybe it was because she was such a good listener. Cristina wasn't going to interrupt; she would listen to every single word you said. Then she'd give her opinion—her truthful opinion. She wasn't the type to tell you what you wanted to hear. She'd give you the bitter truth, and sometimes it was really bitter.

Cristina opened a door to my heart that had been closed

for a long time. She had to pry it open, because even though the door was unlocked, it had been glued shut.

I told her some of the secrets I'd carried around inside me for years. I told her about the false confidence I projected so that people couldn't see my real, damaged self.

I told Cristina about having been molested, feeling rejected and being considered "less than" all my life. I confided in her all the other hurts, large and small, I felt.

Cristina told me that it was okay to hurt, I had reasons to feel that way. She said it was okay to be unsure of myself and insecure, because everybody has those same feelings, to some extent. She helped me see that just because bad things had happened to me, it didn't mean I was an undeserving person.

I felt a great weight lift from my spirit after I unburdened myself to her. I finally could accept who I was and what I represented. For the first time, I became comfortable with being me. I knew I could accomplish anything and everything just being me.

I was okay!

Until then, I had never been able to realize, or accept, that fact. I was okay. I had been so blinded with pain—by the hurt and humiliation I had gone through and the mistrust I felt—that I had never been able to communicate in a totally honest manner.

After I got all that stuff off my chest, I was able to start building healthier relationships and friendships. Before then, I only had friends on a superficial level. People weren't friends with the real me, they were friends with the person I created to protect the real me.

That's also when I began to feel confidence. Not the manufactured confidence I created as part of the front I put on, but real, genuine confidence.

Cristina also helped me close the communications gap with my Parma teammates. She taught me how to express the real me. Most of my teammates thought I was selfish and inconsiderate, even arrogant, but that wasn't the case.

I'm not that type of person and never have been. Yes, I am intense about winning, but I'm a team player—to the max. The team always comes first.

Cristina taught me how to get that message across. She helped me learn to say the right thing, in the right tone, at the right time, that better expressed my true meaning.

And when I made a mistake or did something wrong, Cristina let me know it. She'd give it to me straight. There were times I'd go home angry at her, but I knew she was always in my corner. If she told me I was dead wrong about something, chances were I was.

Around the same time, I had begun coaching a team in Parma for girls age twelve and under (I later coached a boys team as well). Two of my players were the Zinelli sisters, Elena and Chiara, who lived in Monticelli, a neighboring town some twenty-five or thirty minutes away.

The Zinellis have stayed in touch with me through the years. I recently got a letter from their mother, Maria Chiara, who told me that Elena has entered law school and Chiara is in medical school.

Not that I'm starting to feel old or anything. It's just that we're all growing up. Which is something, with Cristina's help, I did a lot of in Italy.

Chapter Eighteen

Blame It on Barcelona

My last experience with the U.S. Olympic team—for now, at least—came in Barcelona in 1992.

That was the year the United States should have won the gold medal in women's basketball. Should have, but didn't.

It was a terrible experience, one of the worst of my career. We had the best team, without question, but we weren't together as a team.

Because we weren't together, we got outplayed by the Unified Team (made up of members of the former Soviet Union) in the semifinals. The Unified Team went ahead and won the gold medal game by routing China, which had imposing 6-foot-8 center Haixia Zheng. The United States had to settle for the bronze medal by beating Cuba.

We were denied the ultimate prize in sports: the Olympic gold medal. It hurt to lose in Barcelona, but we deserved to lose. We were cocky and arrogant and those are not qualities associated with a winning team.

We thought our talent would be enough to carry us through, but basketball is a team sport and players have to work as a unit. We didn't and we lost. Simple as that.

Basketball is a game that whips you back to reality every time you underestimate your opponent or take for granted that you're going to win. Just because a team has the most talent doesn't automatically mean it will win. We proved that against the Unified Team.

Basketball demands that you believe in yourself and believe in your teammates and all work together. Team chemistry is crucial to success.

In addition to our defeat being a case of overconfidence, we lost our focus. More precisely, we lost our focus by becoming preoccupied with the U.S. men's national team. The original Dream Team.

For the 1992 Olympics in Barcelona, the United States Olympic Committee got together with the International Olympic Committee, the National Basketball Association and FIBA—Fédération Internationale de Basketball, the sport's governing body worldwide—and allowed, for the first time, NBA players to compete.

The Dream Team had the greatest collection of talent ever assembled on one basketball squad—from Michael Jordan, Magic Johnson and Larry Bird to John Stockton and Karl Malone, from Clyde Drexler, Scottie Pippen and Chris Mullin to Patrick Ewing, Charles Barkley and the rest. Understandably, the Dream Team received a lot of media attention and hype.

Not just in America, or Barcelona, but worldwide.

The red-carpet treatment the Dream Team received leading up to and during the Olympic Games had a negative impact on the U.S. women's team. Some of our players started focusing less on winning the gold medal and more on the way the members of the Dream Team were being treated, which was like royalty.

For example, the U.S. women's team stayed in the Olympic Village; the Dream Team stayed in a luxury hotel. The U.S. women's team traveled on a team bus; the Dream Team was chauffeured around in limousines. Differences like that got under the skin of some of my teammates. They were envious.

The U.S. women's team was supposed to travel to Spain on a commercial flight. The Dream Team had its own private charter flight. We wound up flying to Barcelona with them, but the original plans remained an issue with some of my teammates.

I kept my focus on the job, which was to play basketball and win a gold medal. But some on the U.S. women's team forgot why we had all played so hard for so many years: because we love the sport of basketball.

The love of the game is what carried the U.S. national team to victory at the Goodwill Games and World Championships in Moscow in 1986, establishing America's women as the best in the world. We had to put up with the bad travel, bad hotels, lousy service and inedible food, but we hung in there and won because we loved basketball. And because we wanted to represent our country in the best possible way.

In 1992, however, the majority of players on the U.S. women's team forgot why we play this game and were more concerned about comparing the treatment they were getting to the men's. They were jealous that the Dream Team had its own T-shirts (one of the hottest-selling items before and after Barcelona) and we didn't. They were jealous about the Dream Team's endorsement deals and the revenues the players were generating.

Even our coach, Theresa Grentz, got caught up in the comparisons between our team and the Dream Team. She, too, became upset that we were treated "less than" the American men.

I couldn't try to tell my teammates to get their heads on straight. I wasn't a leader on the team, just another role player. My teammates wouldn't have listened to me.

On the plane ride to Barcelona, the Dream Team sat up in the forward compartment, which had the big, swivel NBA-type seats. The women's team rode in the back of the plane and sat in standard passenger seats. (Hey, at least the seats were leather.)

Some of my teammates stayed in their seats and pouted the whole flight. No me. I knew this was a once-in-a-lifetime opportunity. I went up to the forward cabin and said, "Hey, fellas, what's going on?"

All the Dream Teamers were nice and friendly. The guys talked to us and signed autographs. I remember Clyde Drexler and his wife were busy changing diapers. Larry Bird sat quietly with his wife. He seemed almost shy. Scottie Pippen was the real energetic one, moving around and introducing himself to everyone and saying, "How y'all doing? What's up? What's up?"

I remember sitting around and watching Michael Jordan, Magic Johnson, Charles Barkley and Scottie playing cards. Charles Barkley was the center of attention. He's Mr. Personality.

We didn't see the Dream Team again after the plane landed in Barcelona. They won the gold medal, of course.

The silver lining behind the Barcelona experience was that the top executives of the NBA got to see firsthand the growing interest worldwide in basketball. And in *women's* basketball.

I think that opened some eyes. I doubt if many of the NBA brass had paid much attention—if any—to women's basketball before Barcelona.

But, being the shrewd marketers they are, the NBA people probably figured that if women's basketball could be a huge success in Europe, Asia and South America, why not in the United States?

After Barcelona, I believe the infrastructure was slowly and steadily put into place to develop a women's professional game in America.

I had maintained all along that for women's basketball to reach its full potential in America, it would need the backing of the NBA. Those people are geniuses; they have the blueprint for how to build a professional league.

People in women's basketball worked off that blueprint for the next several years, and by 1995, USA Basketball had put together the women's version of the Dream Team. The U.S. national team, which included Lisa Leslie, Sheryl Swoopes, Teresa Edwards and Dawn Staley, among others, spent the year leading up to the 1996 Olympic Games in Atlanta playing an international schedule of exhibition games.

Besides prepping for the 1996 Games, the U.S. national team was, in effect, conducting a test market to assess the possibility of a women's professional league. As the national team steamrolled to 60 straight wins, culminating with a gold medal performance at the 1996 Games, all systems said "Go!"

Naturally, I got overlooked for the women's Dream Team. I wasn't invited to participate. It was the same old story of my life: overlooked and underappreciated.

The people at USA Basketball told me the emphasis for the 1996 Olympic team would be on athletes who had played for the U.S. national team in the preceding three years. I wanted to shout, "Wait a minute! What about people who have been playing for the national team for nearly *ten* years?"

In my opinion, it was unfair and unjust for the committee that selected the 1996 Olympic team to overlook so many veteran talents. Granted, it's a moot point because the U.S. women's team won gold.

What we've been learning from the WNBA experience is that many women play their best basketball after the age of thirty. The U.S. Olympic team chosen to participate in the 2000 Games in Sydney, Australia, should be selected on the basis of talent, period. Age shouldn't enter into the decision. Our twelve best women players should be on the team headed Down Under.

Chapter Nineteen

Stepping Up

I've learned many lessons from my mother, one of the most important of which is that you have to be ready to step up when your family needs you. She spent a lifetime stepping up.

My family needed me to step up in 1992–93 for my nephew Tyrone. Tyrone had started first grade in the inner city of Los Angeles and was immediately labeled a problem child. His teachers reported he didn't pay attention in school. Instead, he sat in the back of the classroom creating problems and being disruptive.

That didn't sound like Tyrone to me. I had been around him enough to know he was a great kid.

But instead of addressing his problems, Tyrone's teacher stuck a label on him: troublemaker. She decided he was a bad kid with a terrible family background, so she figured she'd stick him at the back of the room and try to teach the other children.

What that teacher didn't know—and didn't make an effort

to find out—was that Tyrone had extremely poor vision. He couldn't see the blackboard. No wonder he didn't pay attention in class. He had no idea what was going on.

I kept hearing from my mother and my sister Lisa, who's Tyrone's mother, that Tyrone was having trouble in school. I finally convinced them to let me bring him over to Italy. I thought a change of environment might do some good.

I enrolled Tyrone in a private school. The teachers spoke Italian. Cristina helped me make the necessary arrangements and also found a baby-sitter to look after Tyrone if I had to go to practice or out of town for a road game.

After Tyrone's first week at his new school, his teacher called and said Tyrone needed to have his vision tested. Tyrone had told her he couldn't read the writing on the blackboard.

If Tyrone had tried to tell his teacher at an inner-city school he couldn't see, the teacher probably would have thought he was lying. Either that, or making an excuse to get out of doing his schoolwork.

That's the prevailing attitude in the ghetto; people expect the worst in almost every situation.

The eye exam revealed that Tyrone was almost blind. He could see only the big E at the top of the chart. I immediately had him fitted for glasses.

Wouldn't you know, that little boy became an outstanding student. Tyrone learned to speak fluent Italian and learned English as a second language. He showed a real aptitude for math. He was a whiz at addition, subtraction and his multiplication tables.

That troubled boy who sat at the back of the class in Los Angeles, who would never amount to anything, who would probably be a special education student—that same boy became a good student in Parma.

The next year, 1993–94, I brought both Tyrone and his sister, Antonisha, with me when I returned to Parma. They are two years apart in age, and they wanted to be together. Antonisha went to preschool while Tyrone attended second grade.

The kids got along great with their Italian classmates and made plenty of new friends. They bonded with the Bertolazzi children. Julia and Tyrone became real tight, as did Matteo and Antonisha. Cristina helped me with "mommy" duties like getting them ready for school, buying supplies and helping with homework.

It was a good learning experience for all of us.

Being ready to step up, however, isn't the same as being willing to be stepped on.

I found, over the years, that there are some people—sometimes members of your family—who will try to walk all over you and bring you down. There's no bigger star than a fallen star, and if you're not careful, those people will take you back to where you were.

Had I never learned to say NO!—capital N, capital O—I know where I'd be right now. I'd be back in the ghetto. Penniless, broken in spirit and with nothing to show for my basketball experiences but some faded memories.

When I started making a good income playing basketball, some members of my family thought I should support them as well. For a number of years, in fact, I did send as much money as I could back from Italy. But after a while, I realized it was going into a black hole. It disappeared.

I got few signs the money I sent home was helping out or making a difference. It apparently was being spent more on amusement and recreation—and less on useful things, like education. Or clothes for the children. Or books or school supplies.

That experience taught me another lesson: When you give something to people (like money) and they don't work for it, they will never have the same appreciation for it that you do. Never.

The money I earned playing basketball was important to me because I knew how hard I'd worked and how many sacrifices I'd made to acquire it. I had put blood, sweat and tears into becoming a professional athlete. Some people close to me took my success for granted and felt entitled to share in the spoils.

I'm conservative with my money. Cristina helped me learn to put money back for the future. For every $10 I earn, I'll save $5 right off the top. Then I'll spend $3 paying bills and taxes and doing the things you do to live. After that, I might think about spending the other $2 on myself, but if I do, I'll probably feel guilty.

That's just how I am. I don't need a lot of material possessions, or creature comforts, to be happy. I guess the only thing I splurge on is automobiles. I do enjoy driving nice cars.

I also stepped up with another nephew, Tyquon, in 1994–95. Tyquon is Tyrone and Antonisha's little brother. His mother, Lisa, was going through some difficult times around the time he was born (October 12, 1993), and a few months later she asked for help.

On April 15, 1994, when Tyquon was six months old, I started caring for him like he was my own son. I had just come back to Los Angeles from Parma. I had turned thirty-one the day before. I picked up my car, a black BMW 530, which I'd left with my aunt Beverly Bolden. (Beverly's not really my aunt, but we're such good friends she seems like a family member.)

Tyquon and I crossed the southwestern desert on Interstate 10 with him in the back strapped into an infant's car seat and me strapped in behind the wheel, listening to Whitney Houston, Mariah Carey and Luther Vandross on the CD player and driving as fast as I could without being pulled over by state troopers.

I stopped in San Antonio to take care of some business matters, like closing my bank account, saying good-bye to Eric Cooper and dropping off the house keys with my Realtor. I was moving to Houston.

The previous summer, I'd visited Monica Lamb (who played at USC and now is a teammate with the Houston Comets) in Houston, which is her hometown. Monica showed me around the city and I liked its pace. Houston seemed to have a little more going on than San Antonio, and besides, I felt ready for a change. The humidity is wicked in Houston, but overall the climate isn't bad. There are plenty of sunny days, which are good for jogging, walking, cycling and just being outside.

Tyquon and I stayed at Monica's until we moved into a four-bedroom house in the suburb of Sugar Land. Sugar Land used to be a company town for the Imperial Sugar Co., but now it's one of the numerous bedroom communities serving the Greater Houston area.

We were alone that first summer (1994) in Houston, but over the next few years our household began to expand. Other members of my family gravitated to Sugar Land. My brother Chucky. My oldest niece, Brenda, who is Drena's daughter. Tyrone and Antonisha, who we call Danielle. Anthony Campbell, who is also Lisa's son. My brother Kenny's two sons, Kenneth and Denecheo Cobbs.

In the summer of 1995, I talked my mother into coming to join us. I'm sure it was difficult for her to pull up roots after living in Los Angeles for thirty-one years, but we wanted her with us. I figured she had worked long enough and hard enough for two lifetimes; it was my turn to carry the load.

I wanted her to be close to her seven grandchildren. As the head of our family—the glue that keeps us together—I knew she would be able to give her grandchildren all the attention and nurturing they needed.

Things reached a point where I realized we had to have

more space, so in the spring of 1998, I moved into a second house in Sugar Land. It's not far from the other house, and I'm able to move back and forth a lot. I keep a close watch on what's going on over there.

And, like my mother did, I insist on plenty of discipline. Homework and chores come first, then play. Nobody gets a free ride. We all pull together.

People sometimes ask me why I would take on the responsibility of looking after seven children, who range in age from five to nineteen. It's because I want to give my nieces and nephews a chance at a bright future. Or just a future, period.

A bright future isn't always possible in the inner city. It's hard to think about the future when you're struggling week to week and year to year just to get by. And there's always the chance that the negative environment will suck you back in. It's happened in our family.

I'm not providing these children with money—and with a nice house in a nice neighborhood with good schools—so that they can be spoiled. I'm doing it so they don't have to start their lives at a disadvantage.

My mother started out at zero, which is as low as it gets. With determination, she raised our family up to a level where I started out at maybe 30 or 40 on a 100-point scale.

Now I'm determined to raise my family to a level that my nieces and nephews don't have any disadvantage. They can start at 100 percent—just like the kids down the street—and so can their children, too.

This is all about me providing the next generation of my family members with an opportunity. This is about me stepping up.

Chapter Twenty

Sunny Sicily

Tyquon celebrated his first birthday on October 12, 1994, in Sicily. I baked him a chocolate cake and decorated our living room with balloons. We were spending the 1994–95 Italian League season in Alcamo, which is located on the western side of Sicily, about an hour's drive from the capital, Palermo.

After seven seasons with Parma, I had decided to move on. The last couple of years there hadn't been as much fun as the first five. My relationship with Coach Rossi was cool at best. As much as I hated to part company with Cristina, Gianni and the Bertolazzi children, Julia and Matteo, who were growing up before my eyes, it was time for a change. We all realized it.

I contacted Bruce Levy, the New York–based agent, to see what he might be able to arrange. Bruce put me in touch with Vito Pollari, the owner and coach in Alcamo, and we worked out a deal.

Sicily represented a perfect change of pace. The weather in

Sicily is balmy and the disposition of Sicilians is as sunny as the skies overhead.

Alcamo is a small city with a relaxed, easy pace and warm, friendly people. Sicilians are real down-to-earth and in no particular hurry. In northern Italy, for example, everyone eats lunch at precisely one o'clock. Show up at 1:01 P.M. and you're late. In the South (as Sicily is referred to), people are so free-spirited they eat whenever they get around to it.

Because the terrain around Alcamo is hilly, people on that part of the island get around mostly on motor scooters, like Vespas (the team had furnished me with a car). Unless you have the calf muscles of an Olympic cyclist, bicycles aren't much of a match for those hills.

We lived in a two-bedroom apartment with a balcony on the third floor of a high-rise. Tyquon and I could drive five minutes and be in the mountains overlooking the countryside, which has a dry vegetation and stunning natural beauty.

Five minutes in the other direction and we were seaside. About fifteen minutes away on the coast is a national park and wildlife preserve, where fishing is prohibited. The water has a deep blue color and is amazingly clear. The beaches are white as snow.

Because the population in Sicily is comparatively sparse, all the countryside has a clean, unspoiled look. The island reminded me of Hawaii, without the tourists or big resort developments.

I befriended several fans of the Alcamo team, who loved women's basketball and never missed any of our games. Among my closest friends in Sicily were—and are—Francesco Ruvello and his wife, Marianna, and their sons, Gaetano and Leonardo.

I was also close to Antonio Ruvello (Francesco's uncle) and his wife, Maria—who became Tyquon's baby-sitter while we were in Alcamo. And Marianna Ruvello's sister Lydia and her husband, Nicolo Solina.

All the adults are professional people, quite intelligent and good conversationalists. They also like to entertain. They frequently invited Tyquon and me out to their country home, where they had big cookouts.

Sicilians, like most Europeans, know how to eat. They would get their grill steaming and cook fresh fish and chicken. They made their own pasta with basil, garlic and other herbs. They enjoyed life to the fullest extent.

If only the basketball in Sicily could have been as pleasant as the people and surroundings. Vito Pollari turned out to be less of a big-time basketball coach than I imagined. In fact, Vito knew next to nothing about the game.

Vito didn't set a good example for the team, either. He ran loose, disorganized practices. Sometimes he didn't even bother to show up for practice. He was lax about making the players train. His casualness about coaching reflected the prevailing attitude on the island.

Alcamo had great fans. They packed into our small gym, which only held about 600 people, like sardines. We regularly attracted standing-room-only crowds of 1,000 or more. Most fire codes in the United States would have prevented such a crowd from gathering in that building, but in Sicily no one cared.

I again led the Italian League in scoring in 1994–95, with a 32.5 point average. But because of the team's lack of organization and direction, it wasn't a satisfying season.

The only bright spot for me was making friends with Eleonora Magadino, Alcamo's point guard. Eleonora and I became instant friends. She was quiet and shy but an extremely hard worker. She liked to stay after practice with me and we'd work on our shooting.

I became like a big sister to Eleonora. We cared about each other as people, not just teammates. She introduced me to her family—her dad was a big fan of women's basketball—and she'd show me and Tyquon around the countryside.

The friendships I made with people like Eleonora Magadino and Cristina Bertolazzi are the kind that last a lifetime. They are what made those years overseas so special and fulfilling.

When Tyquon and I returned to Houston in 1995—the same summer my mother moved to Texas from Los Angeles—I began thinking my professional career had reached its end. I had grown weary of the annual trip overseas. I hated being away from my family for such a long stretch each year. And I was tired of juggling two homes on two continents.

I wanted to start building a career in America, and my first choice for an occupation was coaching. I wanted to give something back to basketball, which has given so much to me and my family.

Still lacking my degree, I enrolled in communications classes at the University of Houston and began talking to UH women's basketball coach Jessie Kenlaw about working with the team. She added me to the staff as a graduate assistant coach.

I loved interacting with the Lady Cougar players. I got to help out with conducting practices because Coach Kenlaw and her top assistant, Kevin Cook (who's now on the Houston Comets staff), spent most of their time out recruiting.

Scrimmaging against the Lady Cougar players that August and September, I suddenly discovered my competitive juices were still flowing. No question about it, I missed playing the game. At thirty-two, I felt too young to walk away.

Meanwhile, I'd been receiving phone calls from overseas. Vito Pollari was begging me to come back to Alcamo and rejoin the team.

What can I say? The lure to get back on the hardwood was so powerful that I gave in. Tyquon and I left for Sicily on October 7, but not before I thanked Jessie Kenlaw for my brief

SHE GOT GAME / **151**

coaching fling. I felt badly about leaving because I really enjoyed working with the players and I loved the University of Houston.

But my heart belonged to round ball.

By the time I got back in the Alcamo lineup, the team had already played five or six games, roughly 20 percent of the schedule. One of the players had been assigned my old uniform number, 14, so I wore number 12 for the remainder of that season.

It didn't matter. I still poured in 35.5 points a game.

During my second season (1995–96) in Alcamo, a friend of mine from Los Angeles, Kennard Johnson, came to Sicily to try out with the professional team in Trapani, a city on the western coast of the island.

Kennard showed up unannounced in Alcamo at one of our games. He'd found out I was playing in the area and arranged for one of the Trapani players to drive him over to see me.

The man who gave Kennard a ride at Alcamo was named Gianluca Castaldini. He was 6-foot-8, handsome and had fair features capped by a great smile. He had big, white teeth.

The three of us went to dinner that night after my game. I talked mostly to Kennard, catching up on old times and mutual friends, but I spoke in Italian with Gianluca just so he wouldn't feel totally left out. I could tell immediately he was witty and had a good sense of humor.

Kennard Johnson never could work out a deal in Sicily and went back to the States. After he left, I kept in touch with Gianluca, just because he was such fun to be around. I drove to Trapani once or twice to watch him play. He came to some of my games.

We were friends, that's it. We didn't date—from the time I showed up in Parma eight years earlier I'd never been interested in dating Italian men—we just liked hanging out. We'd have dinner occasionally or sit around a coffee bar talking. It was no big deal, and besides, Gianluca already had a girlfriend.

Before the season ended, though, our relationship began to deepen. I can't say for sure how or why, but it did. Yet neither one of us thought we had a future, mainly because I was going home to America after the season.

But during the summer of 1996—while the women's Dream Team was bound for Atlanta and Olympic glory—I got hired by a major shoe manufacturer to conduct basketball clinics and exhibitions in Italy. I left Tyquon with my mother in Houston and headed back to Europe.

I hooked up with Gianluca, who was finished with his season and free to travel with me. He accompanied me to all the exhibitions, and we made a few side trips to visit his family in Saronno, Italy, and see our many friends in Sicily.

I had decided by then to return to Parma for the 1996–97 season. I'd been talking with Cristina, who knew I was unhappy in Alcamo, and she passed the word along to Gianni.

I wasn't unhappy living in Sicily, mind you. That part was great. It was just that the Alcamo team didn't have a championship attitude. Vito was too disorganized, and the players, with the notable exception of Eleonora, were too laid-back.

Once I knew I was headed back to Parma, I made a few phone calls and within a matter of weeks, Gianluca's playing rights were shipped from Trapani to Parma. We both had jobs in the North.

Gianluca and I fell in love that year. He and Tyquon really bonded well, and as I got to know Gianluca better I realized he had a sensitive side.

Our lives were in a total state of bliss. We even started talking about getting married. That's when women's professional basketball in America started to take shape, and I began making plans to go home for good.

It's funny how things work out. Had I stayed on as an assistant coach at the University of Houston in the fall of 1995, I would have missed two full seasons of competition by the time the WNBA started in the summer of 1997.

At age thirty-four, having been out of the game that long, I might not have made it back. Certainly not back to the level of play I established in 1997 and 1998.

I believe that God always has a plan for us, even if we can't comprehend what that plan may be. His guiding me away from a great coaching opportunity at the University of Houston and back to Sicily for the 1995–96 season made possible everything that followed.

Chapter Twenty-one

Coming Home

*B*y the middle of 1996, the seeds for women's professional basketball in America that had been planted after the 1992 Olympic Games in Barcelona were ready to sprout.

Popping up were not one, but two separate entities—the American Basketball League (ABL) and the Women's National Basketball Association (WNBA). Talk among prospective players was that the ABL would play a winter schedule—running concurrently with the season in Europe—while the WNBA would be a summer league.

Players would have to choose one league or the other; the standard contracts issued by both the ABL and WNBA prohibited participation in the rival league.

Before leaving to conduct those overseas exhibitions and clinics in the summer of 1996, I got in touch with the ABL. To be honest, I felt offended that no one from the league had contacted me. It's not like I had stopped playing basketball; I was still the leading scorer in the Italian League and one of the top players in Europe.

Apparently, though, the ABL didn't regard me as a premier athlete or project me as a potential star. I told the official I spoke with about my background and expressed an interest in playing in the league. I had heard through the grapevine the ABL was going to be a players league, meaning the players would benefit directly from the league's success.

The ABL already had commitments from several international stars, including Teresa Edwards, with whom I had played on numerous Olympic and U.S. national teams. Before hanging up the phone, I suggested the official talk to Teresa to verify my ability level.

I assumed the ABL people would be hesitant to sign anyone they hadn't seen play, but I knew Teresa could tell them what type of player I am. Her word would have a lot of credibility with the league.

A couple of weeks went by, and I didn't hear back from anyone. So I called the ABL office again and was told that no one could reach Teresa because she was on tour in Australia with the women's Dream Team. But, the ABL official told me, "We'll be more than happy to invite you to our tryout camp. All you have to do is pay the application fee."

Thanks, but no thanks.

I knew I didn't want to play in a league that had no respect for my game. It wasn't like I was an unproven veteran or a rookie trying to break into pro basketball. Besides, I was under no pressure to sign. I already had a contract for the 1996–97 season with Parma.

When I went back to Italy that fall, I started looking into the WNBA as a possible employer. I called Rhonda Windham, my ex-USC teammate, who at that time was working in the Los Angeles Lakers front office and shortly thereafter would become the general manager of the WNBA franchise in L.A.

Rhonda assured me that the WNBA was prepared to play its first season in the summer of 1997 and that the league had a solid business plan. Broadcast deals had been worked out with NBC Sports, ESPN and Lifetime Television, meaning the league would receive plenty of national exposure. Great, I said, how do I get involved?

Rhonda told me to put together a player profile and send it to Renee Brown, director of player personnel, at WNBA headquarters in New York. I put all the pertinent information together, faxing a copy to Renee at the league office and mailing her a hard copy. I wanted to cover every base.

It so happened that while I was talking with Rhonda, Renee was in Europe, scouting for prospective WNBA players. It took me several attempts to make contact with Renee, but I finally reached her by telephone after she returned to New York.

"Renee, this is Cynthia Cooper," I said. "I wanted you to know that I'm interested in playing in the WNBA."

"Cynthia Cooper? From Parma, Italy?" she asked.

"That's me."

"Relax, girl," said Renee. "You're on our list of the top sixteen [players]. Where can I send you a contract?"

I put down the telephone and pumped my fist. Yes. Yes. Yes.

As soon as I got off the phone with Renee, after pouring out my gratitude, I placed another transatlantic call, this time to Sugar Land.

"Mommy, I'm going to play in the WNBA!" I shouted into the telephone receiver. "I'm coming home."

"Where are you going to play?" she asked.

"I don't know yet, Momma. I'll find out later."

What mattered more than the identity of my new team was to have the opportunity, finally, to play pro basketball in America. I had waited my whole career for that moment to arrive.

About the same time I was talking to Renee Brown, things starting hopping at WNBA headquarters. On October 23, Rebecca Lobo and Sheryl Swoopes, members of the women's Dream Team, were announced as the league's first two marquee players. Right after that, the league announced the signing of two more 1996 Olympians, Lisa Leslie and Ruthie Bolton-Holifield.

At the end of October, the WNBA announced its eight charter teams—Charlotte, Cleveland, Houston, Los Angeles, New York, Phoenix, Sacramento and Utah. Players didn't know yet where they were going to be performing, but at least they knew the possibilities.

On December 4, 1996, the WNBA announced the signings of four more players with Olympic experience—Vicky Bullett, Michele Timms, Janice Lawrence Braxton and me. Vicky, who was an all-star in the Italian League playing for Cesena, and I were teammates on the 1988 U.S. Olympic team. Michele, who's from Australia and is probably that country's best-known player, had also participated in the 1988 Games in Seoul. Janice and I had a long history dating back to the NCAA tournament when USC clashed with Louisiana Tech. (She was also, you recall, the player whose hand check led to my shattering my ankle.)

With all the player signings being announced, it was becoming clear the WNBA had stockpiled some serious talent.

As calendars turned to 1997, meanwhile, we were having a great season in Parma. For one of the few times during my career in Italy, Parma had several members on the Italian national team. That season I averaged 26.8 points a game, winning my eighth scoring title.

Once the WNBA signed its first sixteen name players, the plan was to assign two of these players to each of the eight new teams. To provide some built-in fan appeal for the franchises, players were assigned on a geographic basis.

For example, because Rebecca Lobo had been an All America at the University of Connecticut and already had a big fan base on the East Coast, she was awarded to the New York Liberty. Another member of the women's Dream Team, Lisa Leslie, was headed to the Los Angeles franchise. Lisa, who played briefly with me in Sicily, had been an All-America at USC in the early 1990s. Her assignment to the Sparks was a foregone conclusion.

I stayed busy trying to lobby Rhonda Windham to get the WNBA to make me the second player named to the L.A. team. It seemed natural from a marketing perspective to have two ex–Lady Trojans in the Sparks lineup. In reality, though, I'd been gone from USC so long nobody remembered me. It seemed like ages since my mother and I drove up to the campus in that battered Ford Pinto station wagon.

On January 22, the WNBA announced player designations, and I learned I was going to the Houston Comets. The other marquee player assigned to Houston was 1996 Olympian Sheryl Swoopes. Sheryl, a native Texan, had been an All-America at Texas Tech University in the early 1990s and led the Lady Raiders to the NCAA championship in 1993. She figured to have great fan appeal in the Lone Star State.

Me? My connection to Texas was limited to the fact that my mother and extended family were living with me in Sugar Land. I was a household name in exactly one household.

The WNBA team rosters began taking shape. On February 27, 1997, the league held a draft of sixteen elite veterans. Houston picked up center Wanda Guyton, another veteran star of the Italian League, and swingman Janeth Arcain, a perennial MVP of the Brazilian League and a member of Brazil's silver medal 1996 Olympic team.

Wanda and I made the first-ever public appearance on behalf of the Houston Comets in March. During the noon hour of National Take Your Daughter to Work Day, we spoke to a crowd of maybe 1,000 parents and daughters in the atrium of the First City Bank building downtown.

At that point, most people in Houston didn't know if the Houston Comets was a softball team, a bowling team or perhaps a local sales force for a household detergent brand. Never mind, we were there to tell them who we were and get them pumped up.

I spoke for several minutes about how the Comets intended to bring an exciting brand of professional women's basketball to Houston. I talked briefly about my own struggles and how my teammates and I planned to become positive role models for the youth of Houston. I said we wanted to inspire young girls to live their dreams and worked in a message, aimed at the daughters, about the importance of getting an education and respecting your parents.

Afterward, Wanda and I stayed around with Tom Savage, who had come in from the Continental Basketball Association (CBA) to direct the Comets' media services, and answered a few questions about the upcoming season. Wanda and I even signed a few autograph requests. It was a beginning for the public awareness campaign the Comets conducted that spring. We circulated throughout the community spreading the word that women's basketball was on its way to Houston.

At the end of April, the Comets hired Van Chancellor as head coach and general manager. He'd had a long and distinguished career at the University of Mississippi, winning more than 400 games in nineteen seasons. From Ole Miss Coach Chancellor brought with him as his assistant coach Peggie Gillom, who is the older sister of Jennifer Gillom, the marquee player assigned to the franchise in Phoenix. He also hired Kevin Cook, the University of Houston assistant coach with whom I had worked briefly in 1995.

On April 28, 1997, WNBA held a draft of college players and unsigned veterans. The Comets had been lucky enough to secure the first pick and we used it to select Tina Thompson, who had been a 1997 All-America at USC.

There was no question Tina had ability and competitiveness. The only question about her was the experience factor. Going from college ball to the professional level represents a big step, and some people wondered if Tina, at age twenty-two, would be giving up too much to WNBA veterans in savvy and know-how. (Tina answered that question emphatically during the WNBA's inaugural season.)

That same day, looking for size, the Comets also selected centers Tammy Jackson and Racquel Spurlock and forward Catarina Pollini, a native of Vicenza, Italy, and one of my friends from the Italian League.

The rosters were almost complete. On May 22, guards Patty Jo Hedges-Ward and Nekeshia Henderson, as well as guard/forward Pietra Gay, were allocated to the Comets. On May 28, the league assigned each team four developmental players.

Ours were guards Fran Harris, Tiffany Woosley, Kim Perrot and Yolanda Moore, who had played for Coach Chancellor at Ole Miss. From that group, Kim Perrot, a lightning-quick guard from Southwestern Louisiana who once scored 58 points in a Ragin' Cajuns game (second most in NCAA history), quickly emerged as a player to watch. Her defensive skills were outstanding.

Our preseason practices in early June were very intense sessions. Comets players were trying to prove themselves while they battled for a spot either in the starting lineup or the rotation of the top eight players. We were all in the same boat—rookie players in a brand-new league. No one knew exactly what her role was going to be.

I put a lot of effort into making a good first impression with the coaching staff. I wanted to get out of the blocks quickly and show what I could do. I've always believed in working hard in practice, because practice habits carry over into games. I'm a big believer that practice makes perfect and that an athlete will play the way she practices. So I gave my all every day.

Coach Chancellor ran tough, well-organized practices. He was very good at striking a balance between being hard on the players during workouts yet easing the tension with his jokes and his colorful Southern expressions.

Coach Chancellor has an accent so thick it's wrapped in magnolia leaves. Players sometimes had difficulty understanding him, especially when he'd say things like "Go up yonder"—which meant "go over there."

For the first month or so, I'd have to translate some of the coach's remarks for foreign players like Janeth Arcain and Catarina Pollini, who'd get strange looks on their faces listening to him.

Coach Chancellor could really get on our cases when we failed to execute the offenses and defenses he was putting in. He wanted to show from the start who was in charge and running the show. He ran a tight ship, and you were either on the boat or you weren't.

It's easy for players to adjust to a coach who's that way, rather than one who is wishy-washy or teeters back and forth.

When Coach Chancellor came down on a player too hard, Coach Gillom was there to pick her spirits back up. She would talk to the player and put her at ease. Peggie would explain the message Coach Chancellor was trying to get across in a different, positive way. Coach Cook, meanwhile, concentrated on breaking down film of opponents, going over offensive and defensive tendencies and preparing game plans and scouting reports.

By mid-June, after a couple of rigorous weeks of training camp and an exhibition game against Charlotte that exposed some of our weakness in the area of rebounding, I was eager for the WNBA's inaugural season to begin.

At the same time, my mother's health weighed heavily on my mind. Back in March, within six weeks of learning that I would be playing in Houston, my mother was diagnosed with breast cancer. Her doctor found a malignant lump in her breast during a routine exam. The lump had already metastasized and spread to her spinal cord. The oncology team at M.D. Anderson Hospital in Houston immediately started Mother on an aggressive chemotherapy program.

I flew home immediately from Parma when I found out about her illness and was with her when the treatments began. Then I returned to Italy and participated in the playoffs. Parma wound up losing to Como, which clearly had the best team in Italy and which had a great defender in Mara Fullin, who gave me as much trouble as any defensive player I faced.

My focus wasn't on the playoffs the way it would have been had my mother been healthy. I was too concerned about her condition to play my best basketball.

Fortunately for our family, M.D. Anderson is widely recognized as one of the best treatment centers in the United States and it's just twenty minutes away from our house. Mother has been receiving the best possible care since this ordeal began.

We both feel so grateful that I was assigned to Houston rather than some other WNBA city. We believe the Lord worked it out so we could be together and provide each other with a shoulder to lean on.

Chapter Twenty-two

Raise the Roof

Right from the beginning of my affiliation with the WNBA, I realized the league was something special. Everything the WNBA did, from showcasing its players to unveiling the team uniforms at a special ceremony in New York, was first class.

It was illuminating for players to see the amount of marketing and promotion the WNBA put in place before the first season began. Ultimately, we knew we had to go out on the court and perform, but we were blown away by the masterful job the WNBA was doing in creating images to sell women's basketball.

The sophistication of the WNBA's approach to marketing and promotions was unheard of in women's basketball. We could tell immediately this was Big Time.

When the WNBA's inaugural season began on June 21, few people around the league had high expectations for the Houston Comets. The prevailing opinion was that we would be fortunate to play .500 ball. Preseason attention had focused on the East and West coasts, with the New York Liberty and Los Angeles Sparks generally regarded as favorites to become the first WNBA champions.

The Cleveland Rockers, another team stacked with size and experience, was a good darkhorse choice.

A big part of the reason people discounted Houston's chances was that one of our marquee players, Sheryl Swoopes, was out on maternity leave. Sheryl gave birth to her son, Jordan, on June 25, just four days after the season began.

But even with Swoopes out of the lineup for the first half of the season, the Comets would not be denied. We pulled together and believed in ourselves. We clawed and scratched and never gave up. The heart and courage we showed game after game began to turn doubters into believers.

The Comets set the tone for the 1997 season right from the start. We went on the road to Cleveland, which boasted a large and physical front line that included Eva Nemcova and Janice Lawrence Braxton. We played smothering defense from the opening tip and raced away to a 50–28 lead at halftime. That took the air out of the crowd of 11,455 and sent many Cleveland fans home early.

I scored 25 points, Janeth Arcain had 16 and Tina Thompson, who had to wear a plastic mask to protect a broken nose she'd suffered in one of Coach Chancellor's hard practices, added 14. We came away with a resounding 76–56 win.

I could barely contain my emotions that night in Cleveland. I remember breaking into goose bumps when I put on my Comets uniform for the very first time. But my emotions ran even higher three nights later when the Comets made their debut at home.

The crowd at The Summit was wild with anticipation. People were jumping around and going crazy. The energy inside the building was infectious and fed on itself.

I didn't play a good game. I was so pumped up playing in front of my family and friends that my first shot barely grazed the rim. My teammates picked me up, though, and we beat Phoenix 70–55. One thing I'll never forget was that Charles Barkley, the Houston Rockets superstar, sent every Comets player a dozen long-stemmed red roses before the game. Our dressing room looked like a florist's shop.

Through a quirk in the schedule, we played the New York Liberty three times in the first seven games, twice in Houston and once in New York. The Liberty won all three. The losses were close—by 2 points in overtime and by 3 and 7 points, respectively—but losses nevertheless.

The Liberty had an experienced team, with international veterans like Teresa Weatherspoon, Sophia Witherspoon and Kym Hampton complementing the marquee player, Rebecca Lobo, who had been NCAA Player of the Year in 1995. The Liberty jelled quickly under Coach Nancy Darsch, and based on those three early-season victories, it seemed like they had our number.

Despite the three losses, I wasn't overly concerned. I didn't think New York had a better team. I knew we had a long season ahead of us, long enough to make up the early deficit in the standings.

New York won its first seven games—five wins coming on the road—and established a clear-cut lead in the Eastern Division (New York, Houston, Cleveland and Charlotte formed the WNBA East in the league's first season; Los Angeles, Phoenix, Utah and Sacramento made up the WNBA West). Based on that fast start, some observers probably thought the Liberty would win the division race wire-to-wire.

My play during the early part of the season wasn't up to my normal level. I was adjusting to the faster pace of the WNBA game, which is more like Olympic basketball than the Italian League. Every player on the court in the WNBA is a great athlete.

I was getting accustomed to my coaches and teammates

while trying to learn my exact role on the team. In Sheryl's absence, it wasn't clear at first who would become Houston's go-to player. We had to sort that out.

In the first few weeks of the season, all the players with international experience were having to adjust to the WNBA ball, which (like the women's college ball) is slightly smaller than the regulation men's basketball. The colorful orange-and-oatmeal WNBA basketball had a slick, slippery feel, which led to a rash of turnovers during some of the early games. It took players time to grow accustomed to the ball. (By year two, the WNBA ball had been modified to give players a better grip and feel.)

I finally figured out that I had to start developing a relationship with the smaller ball, so I went into the gym and spent extra hours, before and after team practice, working on my shooting and one-on-one moves. All of that extra work was aimed at getting a better feel for the ball. It began to pay off in the second month of the season.

Even as I grew more accustomed to the WNBA ball and style of play, I had to deal with my mother's ongoing health problems. There were nights when I sat up with her, trying to provide comfort, trying to take her mind off the pain racking her body. It didn't help matters any that around the same time I began having problems with my fiancé.

Gianluca and I had been together for nearly two years. He had come back with me from Italy. I could sense his growing frustration with the hectic WNBA schedule and the travel demands that kept me from attending to his needs. He started acting jealous and possessive. He seemed to resent all the attention I was getting from the Houston media.

I came home to face a new problem every day. I never knew exactly what would happen next, but I could count on Gianluca to complain about something.

Gianluca was an angel around the children. He was their playmate and pal. In their eyes, he could do no wrong. But Gianluca never gave my nieces and nephews any discipline or direction. For example, if they were jumping up and down on the couch—something they knew not to do—he wouldn't tell them to stop. He'd just let them do whatever they wanted.

Or, if the refrigerator was getting empty, Gianluca wouldn't go to the store and buy groceries. Or even tell my oldest niece, Brenda, that we were running low on food. He would wait until I got home from a game or a practice and dump the situation on me.

"The kids won't stop jumping on the couch," he'd complain. "There's no food in the refrigerator."

Gianluca always made me play the part of the bad guy. I had to be the mean person who did the scolding and chastising, administered the punishment and enforced the rules.

Another thing that annoyed me was that every single chance he got, Gianluca would say something negative about my game. He tried to convince me I wasn't as good a player as I thought, or as some people around the WNBA were beginning to say. I may have had twenty strong points as a basketball player, but all he wanted to highlight, and harp on, were my weak points.

I couldn't quite pinpoint what was undermining our relationship, but I began second-guessing myself, thinking I was doing something wrong. I desperately wanted to work through our problems and get everything resolved. When you love someone, you'll do whatever it takes.

But before I could repair the damage, things came to a head on June 30. We had a team function scheduled at the Hard Rock Cafe after our home game with Los Angeles. It was a long and exhausting game, which we won 71–66 in overtime. I was tied up with media interviews for almost an hour afterward, so rather than wait around, Gianluca drove my mother home.

I didn't get to the Hard Rock Cafe until after 11 P.M. I went into a back room and called Gianluca and asked if he wanted me to bring home some dinner. He was furious. He went off on me. No, he didn't want anything to eat.

I ate quickly and rushed home. I found him sitting outside on the patio, smoking a cigarette. That made me angry because I don't like smoking to begin with, and considering my mother's cancer, I felt he was being insensitive. (Besides, he had quit smoking—or so I thought.)

The first words out of his mouth were "I'm leaving tomorrow." Hearing that, I dropped my game bag on the patio and plopped down in a chair. I knew he wanted to blow off steam.

Gianluca rattled off a list of things I wasn't doing. Not paying him enough attention. Not giving him enough praise and support. Talking to strange men (these were Comets fans, offering congratulations!) behind his back.

He finally stopped and asked, "Don't you have anything to say?"

"I think your leaving is an excellent idea," I calmly replied. "I don't know what we've got going, but it can't be love because it's causing me too much stress."

The Comets had to fly to New York the next day. I left Gianluca sitting on the patio and went inside to pack for the trip. Then I turned out the lights and tried to get some sleep. I couldn't sleep, though. I was too upset.

The next morning, I felt mad at myself because I hadn't made any effort to rectify the situation. I didn't really want Gianluca to leave; I wanted to work things out. I begged him to reconsider. I pleaded with him.

He didn't want to talk about it. He said he was going home and asked me to make him a reservation for a flight to Italy. I told him he was a grown man, he could make his own reservation.

I flew to New York that afternoon, crying the whole way. As soon as the Comets checked into our hotel, I called him again. He was still adamant about leaving for Italy. I cried some more.

We lost to New York at Madison Square Garden on July 2. I called him immediately after the game. Was he still planning on going? Absolutely. His mind was made up. It was final.

I came to grips that night with the fact that our relationship was over and I'd have to move on. When we returned to Houston the next day, I was shocked to find Gianluca still at the house.

"We should try this again," he said, trying to offer an apology for what he'd put me through. "I think we should talk."

I almost laughed out loud. "What are you doing here? You've been saying for three days you were leaving. Get your stuff together and go."

Gianluca went. He tried several times after that to reestablish our relationship, but it's like I said before: When I close a door in life, I try to keep it shut.

Two weeks after Gianluca left, I had a private meeting with Coach Chancellor. It was at the beginning of a two-week road trip and right after we had been blown out in Los Angeles 77–52. Our record had dropped to 7-5, three games behind New York, which was 10-2. I was feeling frustrated by my substandard play. I knew I could play better.

I told Coach Chancellor I had more to give the team and asked him to let me take a bigger role. I was committed to helping the Comets win ballgames and I felt to accomplish that I needed more freedom to create.

He let me go. Coach Chancellor told me, "Coop, play your game"—and hearing those words filled me with confidence. I felt inspired and ready to soar. I was ready to become the kind of player I dreamed about being in America.

It was my time to shine.

In the next three consecutive games, I established career highs and WNBA single-game records. The scoring streak started with 30 points in an 82–60 win at Sacramento; I came back with 32 in a 77–69 win at Phoenix.

My teammates were looking for me to take charge. They

were feeding me the ball in rhythm and at good places on the floor. Against Sacramento on July 25, I erupted for 44 points, including 31 in the second half. (Entering the 1999 season, that remains the WNBA record for points in a game.)

I was on fire. I hit 7 three-pointers in the Comets' 86–76 victory, tying a WNBA record Elena Baranova of Utah had set three days earlier in an upset win at New York.

Two games later, I scored 34 points against Los Angeles. In the WNBA's first season, there were 10 games of 30 or more points; I registered 8 of them.

The team and I were smoking. I had justified the coaching staff's decision to expand my role. My scoring average, which had been around 17 points a game early in the season, shot up to over 20. I finished the season with a 22.2 average, nearly 3 points higher than runner-up Ruthie Bolton-Holifield of Sacramento, who averaged 19.4.

Coach Chancellor noticed another change besides my increased offensive-mindedness. "How's Gianluca doing?" he asked one day in Phoenix during our extended road trip. "I haven't seen him around."

"He's back in Italy," I replied. "Things didn't work out."

"Cynthia, he's a wonderful man. You better do what you can to get him back."

"Coach, you just don't know . . ."

"Listen to me," Coach Chancellor said. "I'm a good judge of character. I know what I'm talking about."

I interrupted him. "Coach, when Gianluca was here I was averaging 17 points a game. Now that he's gone, I'm averaging 30 points."

"Coop, let's leave him in Italy," said Coach Chancellor.

Before we played the Mercury in Phoenix, I flew back to New York and filmed a McDonald's commercial with Teresa Weatherspoon, Michelle Edwards and NBA star Grant Hill.

Coach Chancellor was furious with the league for pulling

me away from the team for a day, fearing such a distraction could hurt my performance, but the WNBA was determined to market its product to as wide an audience as possible. Having the opportunity for a tie-in with a major sponsor like McDonald's meant more than upsetting the feelings of several coaches.

The Houston Comets caught fire in the second half of the 1997 season. We won eight of our first ten games in August, including five in a row. Sheryl Swoopes, post-delivery, showed flashes of her old self with an 18-point outburst against Utah. She followed that with 20 points against Charlotte.

Kim Perrot was playing the best defense in the league. Her ballhawking instincts either forced turnovers or kept opponents from getting into a comfortable offensive rhythm. Tina Thompson had answered any lingering questions about being ready to play at the professional level by demonstrating great versatility and range. Tina played tough defense in the middle and crashed the boards, yet on offense she could work her way out to the perimeter and bury three-pointers.

She also led us in one of the Comets' pregame rituals: chanting "Uh-Oh." Pietra Gay had introduced the ritual. When we leave the dressing area and head down the tunnel into the arena, we start going "Uh-Oh, Uh-Oh" while clapping our hands in rhythm. Tina acts as the ringleader. (Uh-Oh is a signal to our opponents: Better watch out, 'cause here we come . . .)

Tina would wind up making first-team All-WNBA. She also would have been a natural choice for 1997 WNBA Rookie of the Year, except that there was no such award. That's because everyone, in a sense, was a rookie that year.

Even the veterans like me.

The winning streak in early August enabled us to overtake New York. The Liberty lost seven of eight games at one stretch in August, squandering what once had appeared to be an insurmountable lead.

New York still had a chance to catch us at the end of the season until the Liberty lost a 72–71 heartbreaker at Cleveland on the next-to-last day of the season. When Rockers guard Michelle Edwards buried New York by hitting a three-pointer at the buzzer, we clinched the Eastern Division crown.

As intense as the competition had been during the WNBA's first season, the energy level on the court was matched by the excitement in the arenas. WNBA games became an event, a happening. None of us had anticipated that women's basketball would be such an immediate success or have such a huge impact.

But it did. In cities like New York, Houston, Charlotte and Phoenix, where Mercury coach Cheryl Miller sparked the whole city with her enthusiasm and fire, the WNBA became a hot ticket.

Everywhere we traveled, WNBA players could feel the buzz. Our games represented great family entertainment. Our fan base wasn't like the NBA's, which draws mostly a male, corporate crowd. Our games were attended by men and women. Girls and boys. Parents and children.

Many people who flocked to our games were relative newcomers to basketball who didn't follow the NBA closely. Some of our fans didn't follow the NBA at all. They were wholeheartedly WNBA fans.

League officials had projected average per-game attendance in the 1997 season at roughly 4,000. Instead, it was closer to 10,000—9,669 to be exact. That kind of widespread support blew everyone away.

The Phoenix Mercury averaged over 13,000 fans a game and never had a crowd smaller than 10,000. When the Comets played in Charlotte on August 16, a WNBA record crowd of 18,937 turned out. It was fantastic!

After my scoring outburst in mid-July, fans around the league started screaming out "Cooooop!" whenever I was introduced at the beginning of a game or every time I made a shot. WNBA fans never ceased to amaze me with their support.

The overwhelming support I received from WNBA fans struck an emotional chord within me. It made me want to play harder for them and never let them down. And the raucous response reminded me how far I had come in basketball and how at long last I had the opportunity to live out my dream.

Every time WNBA fans asked me for an autograph or to have a photograph taken with them—or just to exchange a quick high-five—I was happy to do it. Those are special moments, the kind an athlete won't have all her life.

The 1997 WNBA playoffs were conducted like the NCAA Final Four—single elimination, with two semifinal games followed by a championship game. By virtue of our 18-10 record, we were the top seed and got to host fourth-seeded Charlotte at The Summit. Second-seeded Phoenix, winner of the Western Division, hosted third-seeded New York.

Charlotte hung tough throughout the first half and led at intermission 33–29. They were taking advantage of their size, pounding the ball down low to Rhonda Mapp and Vicky Bullett. They were running their game plan to perfection. We had our hands full and we knew it.

We received a brief scare early in the second half. Tina Thompson and Wanda Guyton collided while fighting for a rebound, and Wanda landed on her head. She had to be carried from the court on a stretcher.

I went over to Wanda and while the medical staff attended to her neck and head, I placed my hand on her leg and said a prayer. I prayed that Wanda would be okay and that the Lord would heal whatever was wrong with her body.

The break in the action while Wanda was being taken off the court gave us time to get our act together. Kim Perrot stepped into the team huddle and said, "Let's start playing like we know how to play." That showed a lot of leadership on Kim's part and we responded. We took our defensive intensity to a higher level.

Tammy Jackson came off the bench to replace Wanda and did a great job in the paint. Janeth Arcain had a double-double performance (15 points, 10 rebounds). We outscored Charlotte 41–21 in the second half and won going away.

I finally heated up and finished with 31 points, including 4 three-pointers. By then, I had started "raising the roof" after hitting clutch shots. It had become the trademark gesture around the league.

Let me set the record straight: Kim Perrot raised the roof—pushing her arms upward to incite the crowd to make so much noise that they blow the roof off the building—before I did.

The first time she raised the roof, early in the season, I thought, hey, that's pretty cool. So I sort of borrowed it from Kim. She doesn't mind.

In the other semifinal, New York traveled to Phoenix and shut down the Mercury 59–41. Phoenix couldn't throw it in the ocean that day, hitting only 15 of 67 shots, or 22 percent. It's not supposed to get that cold in the desert, but the Mercury players were frigid. No one on the Phoenix team reached double figures.

We faced the Liberty in Houston two days later, and I had a calm and serene feeling before the final game. I wasn't nervous at all. I knew how much the Comets had grown and matured since those three consecutive losses to New York early in the year. In our fourth and final regular season meeting, on August 17 at Madison Square Garden, we had ripped the Liberty 70–55.

I believed we would do it again.

I remember seeing Tom Savage, our media services director, in the clubhouse before the final game. I reminded him about the day the previous spring when Wanda Guyton and I spoke to the crowd at the atrium of First City Bank.

"We've come a long way in five months, haven't we, Tom?"

I said. He nodded in agreement; the whole summer had blown by like a whirlwind.

I think the basis for the Houston Comets' success in 1997 was our team defense. We worked our tails off the whole time. We got in the other teams' faces and stayed there. If offensive basketball is about skill, defensive basketball is about desire; no team in the league played with as much desire as the Comets.

The championship game was decided by our defensive intensity. We kept the heat on the Liberty and forced 15 turnovers, 5 by veteran Teresa Weatherspoon. We held New York to 23 of 60 field goal attempts, or 38 percent. Tammy Jackson filled in for Wanda Guyton at center and had 11 rebounds. Tina Thompson scored 18 points and hit one of her patented threes.

I followed my coach's advice and played my game. I had 25 points, including 11-for-15 at the foul line. I dished out a team-high 4 assists.

As the buzzer sounded and our 65–51 victory was complete, the heavens opened up and started raining confetti and streamers and balloons. Players danced around on the court, hugging and kissing. I went running around the perimeter of the court exchanging high-fives with Comets fans.

I loved them. They had been there all season; they stuck with us even when our record was barely over .500 and our goal was just to sneak into the playoffs somehow.

WNBA president Val Ackerman presented the championship trophy to Comets owner Les Alexander (who also owns the Houston Rockets). Then she gave me a trophy as the playoff MVP. I shared the glory with God, my teammates and my own MVP, my mother.

Four days later, we had a parade in downtown Houston to celebrate our championship season. In front of several thousand Comets fans gathered at City Hall, I performed this rap, written by my godbrother, Eric Cooper, at the beginning of the season:

Chorus:
The WNBA is coming to your town
From the East to the West Coast we break it down
The WNBA is coming to your town
So bow down.

We got next as we flex on the hardwood decks.
It's not the size of our checks or the gender or the sex.
It doesn't matter I'll serve you like a fish upon a platter,
Male, female, tall, thin or even the fatter
Hanging on the rim like a Shaquille shatter
Rat ta tat tatta I'm the B-ball master
I'll break you off with 25 in the first quarter
Yes it's a slaughter they call me law and order.

I'm doing push-ups while the competition's eating
Running at the beach while you're getting your beauty sleep
Shooting 500 Js every single day
All I got to say is girl you better pray
Can you feel me
Or better yet can you deal with me
I'm the worst nightmare that you will ever see
So if you are afraid of Freddy
You better not go to sleep
'Cause the WNBA is on the creep.

(REPEAT CHORUS)

When the WNBA's first season tipped off, people wondered who I was and what I had to contribute. By the end, people were holding up MVP signs and chanting "Coop! Coop! Coop!"

How did that feel? Super.

Chapter Twenty-three

The Fame Game

By the beginning of September, I found myself in unfamiliar territory—I was being treated like a celebrity in my own country. For the first time in my career, I had stepped out of the chorus line and taken center stage.

Shortly after the 1997 season concluded, the WNBA brought me to New York for a media blitz. I did a dozen or so newspaper and magazine interviews, one right after another, and then appeared on Rosie O'Donnell's and David Letterman's TV shows.

What a trip! Rosie O'Donnell is more than a casual fan of women's basketball and really knows the WNBA game and players. She has a great way of making her guests feel right at home on the set. Rosie is vivacious and funny, and the way she conducts interviews reminds me of a friendly chat between neighbors.

David Letterman was also warm and gracious. People had told me he could be a tough interviewer, but he made me feel at ease. Like Rosie, he's extremely intelligent and quick-witted. They are engaging, resourceful and know how to keep a conversation moving.

I was nervous before each of the tapings. I had appeared on TV talk shows before, but never shows of that magnitude. I paced around in the waiting area, worried and hyper about what I was supposed to say.

Finally, I told myself, "Just be yourself, Cynthia. And when in doubt, talk about basketball."

I shouldn't have been so worried. The interviews with Rosie and Dave went smoothly. When they asked me about the impact the WNBA is having on contemporary sports, I said that in addition to providing an exciting style of basketball for fans, the WNBA serves to inspire little girls.

"I think we're showing that girls can live out their dreams, if they set their mind to doing something and don't put limits on themselves," I said.

I wore a pantsuit for Rosie's show, with a mustard jacket and leopard-patterned blouse over black pants. For the Letterman show, I wore a black pin-striped suit jacket with a long skirt. The studio was freezing, so I never took off the jacket.

I was trying to make a statement, because I think it's important for WNBA players to project the image of athleticism on the court and femininity off the court. Some girls are leery of playing competitive sports because they're afraid of being labeled too masculine.

That shouldn't be the case, and besides, the pressures of society certainly aren't the same as when I was growing up. In the past twenty years, I think most everyone has accepted the idea that women can be competitive and assertive—not just in sports but also in business and other areas of life—without compromising their femininity.

When I was growing up, my involvement in athletics didn't just keep me off the A-list of girls to date, it kept me off every

list, period. Boys wouldn't look at girl athletes as anything
other than friends. A generation later, attitudes have changed.
Many men who would never have looked twice at female athletes now find themselves attracted to us. They respect our ac-
complishments.

As far back as USC, when I met the McGee twins, I learned
that just because a woman athlete spends part of her day training and sweating and being aggressive, it doesn't mean she
can't be a lady afterward. While I enjoy running around in casual attire, I can get sharp, too. I'm as comfortable in cocktail
dresses and spike heels as I am wearing Nike sneakers and
sweats.

The success of the 1997 Houston Comets and my growing
celebrity created ripples in the endorsement arena. In the wake
of our WNBA championship, I signed to become a spokesperson for General Motors.

General Motors is one of the WNBA's marketing partners.
I had introduced myself to GM executive Dean Rotondo back
in May in New York, when the WNBA team uniforms were un-
veiled. "I'm Cynthia Cooper and I'll be playing for the
Comets," I told him. "You guys should consider signing me.
When I go out there on the court, I'm pretty good."

I gave him my credentials and best sales pitch.

Dean left me his business card and told me to call. I did.
But I didn't hear back, and I figured I was getting the brush-off.
GM already had two WNBA players under contract, Lisa Leslie
and Rebecca Lobo, and apparently they didn't need another.
By the end of the season, though, with the Houston Comets on
the brink of the championship and me on the way to being
league MVP, General Motors began calling.

I signed a contract to become a spokesperson for GM's
Concept Cure Program, which promotes public awareness
about breast cancer and raises funds for breast cancer research.

I also make speeches and public appearances for GM and attend company events.

To help me prepare for life after basketball, General Motors has me involved with an internship program; I work with various management teams on advertising, marketing and communications issues. I'm also scheduled to work with a local GM dealership in Houston to get practical experience generating leads and selling cars.

GM has also put me through media training, which has proven invaluable in helping me spread my message to youth about living your dream and accepting no limits. I'm also going to handle some broadcasting work for GM, working with Eli Zaret, a Detroit TV personality who produces and hosts the popular *Locker Room* show.

One eye-opening experience I've had working with General Motors was learning how major sponsors select athletes to represent specific products and brands. I was intrigued by the depth of research and the amount of discussion that goes into such a decision.

I saw how brands are targeted to various demographics and how advertisers try to align the image of certain athletes with specific products and brands. (For example, GM positions the Buick Regal as the car for the supercharged family. I have done two Buick Regal commercials. And yes, I have a supercharged family.)

I also came to realize how important television is in GM's marketing scheme. The fact that the WNBA received so much TV coverage made it an attractive package to sponsors.

I also attended a cocktail reception in New York that fall where Rosie O'Donnell joined GM's Concept Cure team. She movingly talked about losing her mother to breast cancer. On a lighter note, that night I showed Rosie how to raise the roof.

I've since developed a great relationship with GM executives like Phil Guarascio, who's vice president of advertising and marketing; Dean Rotondo, director of marketing alliances; and account director Matthew Pace. They're all great guys. What I like most is how General Motors has made me feel more like a family member than a business associate or an endorser who's under contract. The GM people have really taken me under their wing, so to speak, and they really care about me as a person.

Shortly after signing with GM, I extended my endorsement deal with Nike. I had originally signed a two-year contract in December 1996, right after it was announced I would be joining the WNBA.

Rhonda Windham had mentioned to a Nike representative, Raye Pond, that the company might want to establish a relationship with me. I talked with Raye and expressed an interest in endorsing Nike products. She put me in touch with Sandi Bittler, who handles the company's contract negotiations with pro athletes.

Sandi offered me what she called the "standard terms" for Nike's first-time endorsers. "I'm not going to quibble over a few thousand dollars here or there," I responded. "But after you've seen me play and have a feel for what I bring to the game, you're going to come back to the table and renegotiate."

Sandi said she liked my attitude. And she assured me that if I proved to be one of Nike's top athletes, I would be compensated as one.

I guess Nike liked what it saw from me during the 1997 WNBA season, because Sandi Bittler came back that fall and renegotiated a new three-year contract, which runs through the 2000 season. Nike also began developing my own shoe, the Air Shake 'em Up. We'll be introducing another new shoe— tentatively called the C-14—in 1999.

After its inaugural season, the WNBA sent a team of top players to Europe for a two-game exhibition in mid-October. I was among the ten players selected, along with fellow first-team

All-WNBAers Tina Thompson, Lisa Leslie and Ruthie Bolton-Holifield.

Also on that trip with us was Nikki McCray. Nikki was coming over to the WNBA from the ABL, where she had been that league's MVP during the 1996–97 season while leading the Columbus Quest to the first ABL championship. The WNBA assigned Nikki to the expansion Washington Mystics for the 1998 season.

We played against national teams in Germany and Italy. We beat the Germans in Bonn, the Italians in Como. The highlight of the trip for me was getting to visit with the Bertolazzi family and other close friends from Parma, who traveled up to Como to see me play. We got caught up on old times.

Another highlight was the enthusiastic welcome—primarily thanks to satellite TV—WNBA players received abroad. Women's basketball fans in Germany and Italy, who routinely watched our games on an international feed, were busy raising the roof.

In Germany, the PA announcer had a great technique for interacting with fans. When one of the German players scored a basket, the announcer would call out her first name and then the entire crowd, in unison, would roar her last name. (For example, he would say "Marlies" and the fans would yell "Askamp.")

The WNBA players thought that was really cool. We talked about taking that back to our teams in the United States. I remember Lisa Leslie said she was going to see to it the Los Angeles Sparks started doing that same thing.

I had flown to Europe for the two-game exhibition directly from Brazil, where I had been playing in the Brazilian League. In the fall of 1996, I signed a contract to spend the 1997–98 season in Brazil as a kind of insurance policy. At the time, I had no idea I would have such a great first season in the WNBA.

I spent less than two months in Brazil. When I got word that my mother's condition was getting worse, I came home to Sugar Land to be with her. She takes precedence over everything.

I was playing pickup ball at Fonde Recreation Center in Houston (where many of the city's best players, amateur and pro, like to congregate) that fall when I ran into a typical case of male chauvinism. It's amazing to me how many men automatically assume they are better basketball players than women.

They make that assumption based exclusively on the fact they belong to the male species. Some of these guys may never have played organized basketball in their entire lives, some may only have played a little intramural ball in college, but, hey, they're men, so they must be better. No questions asked.

I was sitting on the side of the court, dripping with perspiration after a fairly strenuous shooting session, when I overheard a conversation between two Fonde regulars.

I don't know what triggered the comment, but one of them said: "Ain't no woman ever going to beat me, man. All I gotta do is back a woman down on the post and shoot over her. On defense, I'll get physical with her. Women can't play no basketball. That's why they use that small ball."

I piped up. "You really believe you can beat any woman? If that's right, let me ask you this: Do you think you can beat me?"

"Aw, yeah, no problem," he said. "Look at me. I'm bigger and stronger than you. I can back you down." He stood about 6-foot-2 and had an athletic build, if slightly overweight.

"Okay," I said. "Let's play a game of one-on-one."

"I can't play with that small ball," he protested.

"No, no, no," I said. "I have no intention of playing with the small [WNBA] ball. Let's play with your ball."

We played a game to 11 points, where each basket counts one point and if you make your shot you keep possession. I beat him 11–1. He was devastated.

All his friends on the sidelines began hooting at him. "She took you, man," they teased. "She *used* you."

"Aw, man, I let her win," he groused. "I didn't want to shake her confidence."

Since that day, no man at Fonde Rec has challenged me to a game of one-on-one. They'll sit around and talk the talk—"I can beat you, Coop, I can do it"—but when it's time to play they're not stepping out on the court.

The usual excuse I get is: "No, Coop, I don't want to show you up." Right.

My cousin Gary Cannon, a former football player, used to have the same sort of bias against women's basketball. The first year of the WNBA, he came to only a couple Comets games. When I took him out to the gym and beat him one-on-one, he suddenly gained a new appreciation for female athletes.

During the second season, Gary and his wife, Deborah, showed up for the majority of our games. He's become a loyal and dedicated fan of women's basketball.

One of the highlights of my first WNBA off season was participating in the Nestlé Crunch All-Star 2ball, which was part of the NBA's All-Star Weekend in New York on February 7, 1998.

2ball is a one-minute competition that involves core skills like shooting, rebounding, dribbling and passing, and requires players to shoot from seven specific locations on the court. Teams score points based on the difficulty of each shot made. 2ball, with its rapid pace, puts a premium on teamwork and timing.

Each of the U.S. cities that has both an NBA and WNBA franchise had a team in the competition. I was paired with Clyde Drexler of the Houston Rockets. Clyde is so cool and smooth that he takes everything as it comes. He's such a performer that when the whistle blows, he just turns on the talent.

We were lousy in the warm-ups. So lousy that Cheryl Miller

came over and put her arms around both of us and said, "Soooo, is this your first time to try 2ball?"

I was nervous, which is unusual for me on a basketball court. I was so keyed up about making a good impression on the NBA crowd that my palms actually started sweating. I couldn't remember the last time that had happened.

Clyde could read the tension in my face. "Coop, settle down," he said. "You're a gamer. You're a player. You'll do fine."

Drexler wasn't nervous. Guys like Glen Rice of Charlotte and Mitch Richmond of Sacramento and even soft-spoken Allan Houston of the New York Knicks were talking some mess, saying they were going to win and wondering aloud why other teams were even bothering to compete. Just to shut everyone up, Clyde kiddingly suggested, "Okay, let's put some money on it." That shut everybody up.

I thought, "Uh-oh. Hold on a minute there. I'm not sure I can be doing that." To be honest, I thought Sacramento would be the team to beat, primarily because Mitch Richmond and Ruthie Bolton-Holifield are such pure shooters.

But Clyde knew what he was talking about. We got in a rhythm. We flowed. We were like poetry in motion. We sailed through the competition, beating Utah's Karl Malone and Tammi Reiss in the final round.

That trip to New York for the NBA All-Star Weekend coincided with the ESPY Awards presented by ESPN. The ESPYs are among the most prestigious awards in sports.

ESPN hosted a gala affair, broadcast live, and I've never seen so many outstanding athletes in one place at one time. It seemed like every big name in the world of professional sports was there—from Ken Griffey Jr. and Tiger Woods right on down the line.

I received the ESPY Award for female basketball player of the year. Roma Downey, the star of *Touched by an Angel*, presented the award. That seemed appropriate, because in my acceptance speech I talked about how my mother and I had been blessed from above.

I was also nominated for Woman Athlete of the Year in 1997, but I lost in that category to soccer star Mia Hamm. I got to meet Mia during the ESPY reception, and she's a dynamic individual in addition to being a great soccer player.

During the off season I also received an Arete Award, which is given for courage in sports. My mother and I attended the ceremony in Chicago. In accepting the award, I thanked the Lord for giving me the ability to perform athletically but pointed out that the truly courageous person in my family is Mary Cobbs.

One of the most thrilling parts of the first WNBA off season was finding out just how closely NBA players follow the women's game. Whenever I attended a Houston Rockets home game, NBA players would offer congratulations on the Comets championship and my MVP award.

When the Chicago Bulls came to town, Michael Jordan sought me out. He called me "Coop" just like we were best friends. When the Los Angeles Lakers were in Houston, I ran into Magic Johnson and he gave me a big hug. "Cynthia, great job," he said, squeezing me tight. Thanks, Magic. When Orlando came to town, Penny Hardaway congratulated me and challenged me to a game of one-on-one when his knee—he was rehabbing after surgery—healed. We need to schedule a makeup date.

I had met Michael and Magic on the Dream Team's plane trip to Barcelona, of course, but I didn't really expect them to remember me. Instead, they acted like we were colleagues and old friends. That showed me how much respect the WNBA had attained within the ranks of professional basketball.

For the Houston Rockets' first home game in 1997, I sent each player a gift basket. I remembered Charles Barkley's grand gesture of sending roses to the Comets players that summer and wanted to reciprocate. One good turn deserved another.

In November 1997, after returning from Brazil, I stepped up my personal conditioning program. I started working with a new strength coach and trainer, Anthony Falsone. We trained at the Westside Tennis Club in Houston, and over the next several months, during which I recovered from arthroscopic knee surgery, Anthony took me to a new level in conditioning.

I had surgery performed on my left knee on December 8, 1997. It had bothered me late in the WNBA season, but I was determined to finish the playoffs no matter what. Comets trainer Missy Leget and I thought the lingering pain was probably tendinitis, which comes from constant wear and tear. We treated the problem as an inflammation.

But my knee didn't improve any that fall, and a Cybex test subsequently revealed I had a tear in the meniscus. I had the surgery performed at Methodist Hospital by team physicians Walter Lowe and Bruce Moseley. Anthony's workout regimen helped speed my recovery.

I've always kept myself in good shape. I've never smoked, taken drugs or had much of anything to do with alcohol. I'm not the type to go to clubs and party. I like to get my rest.

I might sneak a few potato chips in the off season, but my weight seldom fluctuates much from my normal 150 pounds. I'm a firm believer in saying "You are what you eat," so I'm extremely careful about what goes in my body.

Recently, in fact, I've adopted a vegetarian diet. It basically boils down to my belief that meat isn't good for you; our bodies weren't meant to digest meat. Besides, when we cook meat we kill all the enzymes that are supposed to help us. So why eat it?

After my first few weeks of vegetarianism, I felt a bit weak and had trouble with recurring headaches. But my body has since made the adjustment and I've been adding to my diet with Infitrim, a nutritional supplement.

I always get plenty of exercise—even in the off season. I started walking with my mother after her cancer was diagnosed. I walked with one of my nieces when she was having a bit of trouble with her weight. And I've always liked to jog. Jogging is therapeutic for me because it gives me time alone to sort out various problems and issues.

The only time that my physical conditioning suffered was during the summer of 1995, when I attended classes at the University of Houston and assumed my playing career was over. When I returned to Sicily that fall, I learned just how out of shape I was. And I found out that at age thirty-two, I couldn't regain my conditioning as quickly and easily as I could at twenty-five. That was tough.

But not as tough as working out with Anthony, who's been the Houston Rockets' strength coach for the past five years and was hired by the Comets beginning in 1998. He started training me using the regimen of periodization, where periods (or cycles) of extreme exercise are followed by periods of active rest. Periodization became popular worldwide after the success of Eastern bloc athletes, especially weightlifters, in the 1970s.

Under Anthony's supervision, I became better conditioned and more energetic. I was as strong in the final ten minutes of a game as the first ten. I was able to withstand the more physical brand of defense teams threw at me in year two.

Anthony introduced me to concepts like hypertrophy—high-volume weightlifting that builds muscle mass—and plyometrics—exercises and drills that develop explosive movements, like running or jumping or fast movement of the feet.

He concentrated on strengthening weak areas of my body, especially the abdomen, lower back and upper torso. The strongest part of my body was my legs, but Anthony eliminated the imbalance between my hamstrings and quadriceps.

We also spent a lot of hours stretching, adding elasticity to my muscles. A good stretching program will make an athlete more flexible and less prone to injury, and speeds that person's recovery time.

In the spring of 1998, when I wasn't working out under Anthony's watchful eyes I was in Los Angeles making TV commercials.

In one spot—which Anheuser-Busch produced on behalf of the WNBA—I look on approvingly as a couple of guys play a heated game of one-on-one on the playground. I decide to pay them a compliment, "Hey, you guys play like girls."

They look over and say "What?"—then recognize who I am. "Why, thank you," they say.

Tina Thompson and I also made a Nike spot—with the popular sassy little girls. The spot shows me and Tina seated in a diner having a meal, when the girls approach and get on my case about not passing the ball to Tina on the fast break. They demand that I apologize to Tina because "she's money down there."

I also traveled to Florida and recorded a song, "Join In," which became a WNBA anthem. The producer of the session, Chris Perkins, has since become a close friend whom I lean on for support. Those commercials and the recording were really fun to do and added to the league's impact and image. So did another TV spot—a rap I made—to promote Lifetime Television's broadcasts of 1998 WNBA games.

Thanks to Anthony Falsone—who's fun to work with and really knows his stuff—I headed into the 1998 WNBA season in my best shape ever. By far. I had my sights set on helping the Comets make history. We were gunning for back-to-back championships.

Chapter Twenty-four

She Got Game

I remember Carroll Dawson, a former Houston Rockets assistant coach who's now vice president of operations, saying before the WNBA's second season how difficult it would be for the Comets to repeat as champions.

CD, as he's known by everyone, had been on the bench with coach Rudy Tomjanovich when the Rockets won consecutive NBA crowns in 1993–94 and 1994–95 (which changed the nickname of Houston from "Choke City" to "Clutch City"). He had seen firsthand how opposing teams gear up to knock the defending champions off the top.

CD spoke at a Comets team meeting when training camp opened. "If you think you can repeat as champions by playing at the level you played last year—you're wrong," he said. "You'll have to raise your level of play, because teams will be coming after you with everything they've got."

His words proved prophetic. During the 1998 season, Comets players felt like we had a big red X displayed on the front of our jersey. Teams took their best shot at us. Every game was a real battle. A war.

Our opponents played a hard and physical brand of ball against us. They gave me special attention, using more double teams and help defense. They basically said, "We're not going to let you beat us, Coop"—so I had to be patient and get my teammates more involved. I had to try to avoid forcing the action and let things happen within the flow of our offense.

Despite the determination of other teams to unseat us, the Comets won a second consecutive WNBA title in 1998. Houston had a historic season, losing only three games out of thirty.

That .900 winning percentage is the highest in the history of professional basketball—male or female. Major leagues or minor leagues. The highest, period.

For our second season, we switched the starting lineup to accommodate Sheryl Swoopes's return to full-time duty. Sheryl came back in great shape and played like she was on a mission to show everyone what she could do.

She scored 28 points to lead us to a 73–62 win in the season opener against New York in front of a sellout crowd of 16,285 at the Compaq Center (formerly The Summit). She went on to have an outstanding year, averaging 15.6 points and being one of three Comets—along with Tina Thompson and me—named 1998 All-WNBA first team.

To make room for Sheryl at the small forward position, Janeth Arcain moved to the sixth-man role. Janeth's such a terrific athlete and accomplished player that she gave us a spark whenever she came in. She stepped back into the starting lineup when either Sheryl or Tina had to miss a game because of injuries.

Our starting center, Wanda Guyton, played only half of one game in 1998, the opener with New York, before injuring her back. Wanda underwent surgery for a herniated disc and spent the year on injured reserve. (She's recovering well, and we're looking forward to having Wanda back for the 1999 WNBA season.)

The Comets had also lost Tammy Jackson, who had played such outstanding ball in the 1997 championship game, in the expansion draft in February. Approaching the 1998 WNBA season, we lacked both experience and depth at center.

But we received a big boost from newcomer Monica Lamb, who returned to competition after sitting out the 1997–98 season recovering from a knee injury and a broken eye socket. Standing 6-foot-5 and having long arms, Monica gave us the intimidating presence in the paint that we lacked during our first year.

Monica showed she could be a force during an early-season game in Los Angeles. Lamb put up a double-double (14 points and 11 rebounds) and left the Sparks' center, Haixia Zheng, wondering where she went. I remember telling Monica during a timeout, "That's right. You go, girl."

Yolanda Moore continued her development in the post and earned heavy minutes as backup center. Yolanda made four starts during the 1998 season. For additional depth at center, we reacquired Tammy Jackson after she was waived by Washington at the end of June. It was comforting to all of us to have a player with Tammy's ability and experience (she had been my teammate at Alcamo in 1994–95) ready to be called upon.

Besides the additions of Sheryl Swoopes and Monica Lamb, the Comets' starting lineup in 1998 had three holdovers: Kim Perrot at point guard, Tina Thompson at power forward and me at shooting guard.

Kim continued to play top-notch defense and push the pace of our offense. She got off to a slow start offensively, but her shot came around as the season progressed. Tina had another terrific season, averaging 12.7 points and 7 rebounds a game. Among centers and forwards, she's probably the best young two-way player in the WNBA.

I wanted to prove that my MVP award in the 1997 season wouldn't be considered a fluke, that I have some serious game. I backed up my 22.2 scoring average in 1997 with a 22.7 average in 1998 and added assists and leadership to the mix.

There's no doubt I improved from the first season.

The WNBA expanded from eight teams to ten for year two, adding franchises in Detroit and Washington. Houston, Los Angeles, Phoenix, Sacramento and Utah made up the Western Conference; Charlotte, Cleveland, Detroit, New York and Washington formed the Eastern Conference.

Crowds, like the league itself, continued to expand. More and more, we would look up in the stands on road trips and see girls—as well as women—sporting replica red jerseys of the Houston Comets. Numbers like 14 (mine) and 22 (Sheryl's) were as commonplace as sneakers on feet.

If the NBA champion Chicago Bulls were the most popular basketball team on the planet, we were the most popular women's team. Everywhere we went, we played in front of a packed house.

One of the major differences in attendance during our second season was the addition of more male faces in the crowd. Men started to appreciate and respect women's pro basketball. I saw more fathers sitting with their daughters and had more men coming up after games to ask for an autograph or to introduce me to their children. Many of them made the comment how impressed they were with the WNBA's level of play.

I could tell we were making a myth of the male mind-set that girls can't play this game. Men were falling in love with women's basketball. It was remarkable to see.

The Houston Comets began the 1998 season with five consecutive wins. Then came a showdown in Phoenix where we knew going in we'd have our hands full. The Mercury was off to a 3-1 start and figured to be our strongest competition in the Western Conference.

There's not a tougher place to play a road game in the WNBA (unless it's Houston). The crowds at America West Arena are large and rabid, and all the noise and energy elevates the Mercury players. If things ever hit a lull, Phoenix coach Cheryl Miller gets everyone pumped up again.

You have to give Cheryl credit, she could always work a crowd. She has showmanship and flair.

It was a tight game throughout, but Phoenix prevailed in front of 12,622 loud and raucous fans 69–66. Bridget Pettis scored 20 points to lead the Mercury attack. I scored 27 points, and Tina Thompson had 13 rebounds in defeat. We didn't know it then, but the loss foreshadowed events that would unfold at the end of the 1998 season.

After losing to Phoenix, the Comets went on a 15-game winning streak, setting another WNBA record for consecutive victories. We were 12-0 during the month of July. In a game against Sacramento on July 18, I became the first WNBA player to reach 1,000 career points.

After we got off to such a torrid start, one of my main goals became to finish undefeated at the Compaq Center. But that dream was extinguished on August 1, when we suffered our second defeat of the season—and our first at home—to Cleveland.

The Rockers always seem to give us fits. They have a big front line that's hard for us to match up with, and players like Rushia Brown and Isabelle Fijalkowski seem to light up whenever they see us coming.

I'd have to blame that defeat on our poor shooting. I went 5-for-14 from the field, and Sheryl was 6-for-19. The Rockers did a number on the boards, outrebounding us 37–25. Cleveland took a 40–29 lead at the half, and although we tied them at 68–68 in regulation play, they outscored us 6–3 in the overtime.

We reeled off another five straight wins after losing to Cleveland and stood 25-2 when we traveled to New York on August 15. The Liberty had their way with us, winning 70–54. By that point, we already had the home court advantage in the playoffs secured, so we didn't have as much incentive as New York.

The common element in each of our three losses in 1998 was that, for whatever reason, we didn't play together as a team those days. We were too individualistic and didn't stay within our roles. Most of the time, we were able to put aside any differences and focus on one common goal: winning.

It wasn't an uneventful season. Some of the players had difficulty at times adjusting to our various roles. With the help of the coaching staff, we ironed out our problems.

I think Van Chancellor and his assistant coaches—Peggie Gillom and Kevin Cook—did a good job keeping us all focused on winning and not letting team morale break down or get out of whack. We finished with a 27-3 regular season record, so it's ridiculous to say very much went wrong in 1998.

After such a spectacular regular season, we headed into the playoffs as the prohibitive favorites to repeat as WNBA champions. Nothing that occurred in our first-round matchup with Charlotte indicated any differently.

We played some of our best ball in the series opener at Charlotte on August 22, winning 85–71. I led the way with 27 points and four other Comets—Sheryl (17), Kim (13), Tina (12) and Yolanda Moore (10)—reached double figures. Yolanda shot 5-for-5 from the field in 15 minutes of play. We enjoyed a huge 35–20 margin in rebounding.

We came back to Compaq Center on August 24 and closed out Charlotte 77–61. I had 23 points and Sheryl scored 18. Tina Thompson tied her career high with 14 rebounds, and Sheryl set a career high with 13.

The playoff format for 1998 had been changed to best-of-three series for the semifinals and finals. That was preferable to a one-game showdown because it gave both cities involved in the series a chance to come out and support their home team.

What I didn't like was that the format called for a road-home-home schedule for the higher seed team. I believed the higher seeds (like the Houston Comets) had earned the right to begin each series at home. We should have been given a home-road-home format.

After dispatching Charlotte, we faced the Phoenix Mercury. We held a 3–1 edge in the season series, but all the games had been close ones. They had a good, sound concept for how to play us.

Both teams endured poor shooting nights in game one. We hit 32 percent, Phoenix 34 percent. I don't think it was playoff nerves as much as good defense and the fact that shots we normally make weren't going down.

Sheryl struggled with 3-for-14, and Tina was 2-for-8. I shot 11-for-24 and kept us in the game with 29 points.

But Phoenix pulled off a 54–51 thriller after the Mercury's marquee player, Jennifer Gillom, hit a big shot in the last minute. Jennifer, who's known as "Grandmama" to her teammates and around the league (even though she's fourteen months younger than I), is the younger sister of Peggie Gillom.

Jennifer has been a great player internationally for many years, and now folks in America could see her stuff. She's got game, too.

We returned to Houston with the pressure on us. The only positive was that we'd held Phoenix to 54 points in game one. They had the home court and home crowd advantage, and all they could muster was 54 points. We felt we'd be all right if we remained aggressive on defense and got our offense going.

But we didn't. Phoenix outplayed us again in game two, taking a 37–32 halftime lead. They were running our offense better than we were, anticipating our ball movement and beating us to the spot. Nothing we tried seemed to work. They had an answer for everything.

But a funny thing happened with about seven minutes left. Officials with the WNBA started making arrangements for the championship trophy presentation. They even brought out theater ropes, which are used to cordon off the floor.

That was fitting because the Houston Comets were indeed on the ropes. No question about it. Seeing what was happening, Coach Chancellor told us during a TV timeout, "They're getting ready to have a trophy presentation. In *your* house."

Like hell they were. We had plenty of time to mount a comeback. We went back onto the court and got in everybody's face.

Before that timeout, the Mercury had been feeling it. You could see in their faces they thought the WNBA title was theirs. Who could blame them? Up to that point, they had given us a real whipping. Cheryl Miller had even started to lighten up a bit on the sidelines. She was smiling along with her players.

We turned their smiles to frowns. We played such smothering defense that we made it tough for the Phoenix players to breathe. Our defensive pressure brought the Comets fans back into the game, and we went on a 13–0 run to catch up.

Cheryl Miller started coming unglued. She was yelling at everyone—her players, the officials, people in the stands.

I came off a screen and hit a big three that put us ahead by a point. I was too busy pumping my fists and shouting Yes! Yes! Yes! to raise the roof.

But Phoenix didn't fold. Jennifer Gillom hit another big shot to force the game into overtime. We were tied at 66, but the Comets had the momentum after our dramatic comeback.

We outscored Phoenix 8–3 in overtime, and the 74–69 victory squared the series at a game apiece. I scored 27 points to lead the offense, while Sheryl Swoopes and Tina Thompson both had double-doubles.

We had passed the key test of the season. We had responded in the clutch when we looked dead. Now the pressure shifted back to the Mercury. It was Phoenix's turn to face a must-win situation.

The final game was close throughout the first half. We led at the intermission 32–26. But in the second half, we got our running game going and gradually began to pull away.

Final score: Houston 80, Phoenix 71. I had 23 points, while Tina and Sheryl added 18 and 16. Kim Perrot chipped in with 13.

We were WNBA champions again. Incredibly, the standing ovations in the Compaq Center were louder than the year before. Fans celebrated with more enthusiasm and emotion.

So did the Comets players. There had been a lot of pressure on us to repeat. There had been a lot of eyes watching closely to see if Sheryl Swoopes and I could coexist.

I think our whole team wanted to prove that we could play together and win together. We had our ups and downs, but ultimately we went out there and took care of business. We did our job, what we're paid to do: We won another championship for the Houston franchise.

The second WNBA season had been a grueling and exhausting one. Teams played me more physically, and I kept having collisions on the court.

In the first game of the season against New York, I got kneed in the thigh by Sue Wicks. Against Phoenix, I ran into an elbow thrown by Bridget Pettis that left me with a huge black eye. Against Charlotte, I had my cornea scratched by Tora Suber.

On August 7, during a road game against the Detroit Shock, I got kneed in the thigh by center Razija Mujanovic about six minutes into the game. I had to leave the court briefly, but Comets trainer Missy Leget got me iced down and then stretched out, and I got back into action. Missy does a tremendous job helping Houston players combat nagging aches and pains. She's a big reason we're able to stay reasonably healthy during the 30-game schedule and playoffs.

I finished the game with 34 points (in 33 minutes), tying my 1998 high. That game was the first chance my General Motors family members had to see me play in person; I didn't want to disappoint them.

In our very next game, back home against Charlotte, I got creamed by Sharon Manning, one of the nicest girls you could ever hope to meet. I was going over a pick and she didn't see me coming; her shoulder smacked directly into my jaw. I was knocked woozy.

Missy Leget took me into the dressing room, and the medical staff—Drs. John Divine, Walter Lowe and Bruce Moseley—gave me some neurological tests to make sure I was all right. I couldn't wait to get back on the court and kept begging the doctors to let me play, but they kept telling me to relax and calm down. I finally returned to action in the second half but played a season-low twenty-two minutes. Still, I managed to score 20 points.

Then, in the opening round of the playoffs against Charlotte, I got banged in the knee on three separate occasions. It wasn't just the Sting players who were dishing out the punishment, either; one of the collisions occurred with my teammate Tina Thompson. By the end of the game my entire leg had swollen.

The bumps, bruises and mini-concussions notwithstanding, the second WNBA season was a sweet and gratifying one. We had stayed on top of the mountain long enough to enjoy the view.

Chapter Twenty-five

Getting Better

Shortly after we won our second WNBA championship, I took the time to reflect on the 1998 season. I realized what a special achievement it had been for the Houston Comets to repeat as champions in such a talented league, with so many great players.

As Carroll Dawson warned us at the beginning of the season, repeating wouldn't be easy. It wasn't. We learned that one of the axioms of sports—a championship level is harder to sustain than attain—is indeed true.

I also thought about how blessed I had been to play on two NCAA champions, a gold medal U.S. Olympic team and now two WNBA champions. Some outstanding basketball players go through an entire career and never even get to the playoffs, much less win an outright championship.

Houston's second title was a blessing, but I can't say it was a shock or surprise. My teammates and I worked, planned and did everything in our collective power to accomplish that feat.

Anything short of a championship would have been a bitter disappointment.

I think the main ingredient that has set the Houston Comets apart from our competition in the first two seasons of the WNBA has been our work ethic and commitment to success. We've constantly pushed each other to improve. Day in and day out, month in and month out, we've found ways to get better.

Now the challenge before us is to continue to improve. We have a reasonable chance to win a third consecutive WNBA title in 1999 if we don't become complacent or self-satisfied. We must stay hungry and not lose any of our desire. Otherwise, there is a howling pack of teams ready to overtake us.

One of the dominant themes of the Cynthia Cooper story is self-improvement. The reason I emerged as the leading player in the WNBA during its first two seasons is that I've spent a lifetime getting better.

From USC to Spain, from Italy to Sicily, right on back to the U.S.A., I've become a better basketball player every single year.

When I needed to develop my dribbling skills with my left hand, I did. When I needed to develop more range and consistency with my jump shot, I did. When the time came to add a three-point shot to the repertoire, I went out and worked on that.

After sharpening my offensive skills, I continued to work on other facets of the game: passing better; reading the court better; playing better individual and team defense.

I was a better player in the second season of the WNBA than in the first. No question. And I expect to have an even better season in 1999.

I'm smarter and more mature. I've learned what it takes to compete at a championship level in the WNBA. I'm already busy thinking about areas in which I can improve—like interacting with my teammates better, reading defenses better and adding some new offensive moves.

My strength on offense is that I'm a complete player. I can drive left or right, shoot the pull-up jumper or bury the three-point shot. I can create scoring opportunities for myself and my teammates. My weakness is that sometimes I don't make the best decision on when and who to pass to or whether I should pull up for a jumper or drive all the way to the hole. I'm working on making better decisions, as well as playing better defense and raising my field goal percentage.

I see no reason why—if I continue to train hard, eat right and am fortunate enough to avoid serious injury—I can't be a better player at age forty than I was at age thirty. That's certainly my intention.

That same general principle—getting better—applies to everyone. No matter where you are in life, you can do a better job. You can learn new and better ways of doing the things you do.

If you're a teacher, you can prepare better lesson plans. If you're a doctor, you can find new ways to treat disease. If you're an entrepreneur, you can bring new products to the marketplace.

Artists can create better art. Scientists can expand the realms of science. Politicians can provide better public service. We all have the capacity to accomplish more—and rather than letting that fact overwhelm or intimidate us, it should motivate and inspire us to grow.

To *get better.*

It's been said many times that life is a journey—not a destination. We never arrive. We just keep growing and moving forward and having new experiences. It's applying the knowledge and know-how we gain through these life experiences that allows us to grow in all phases of our being—mental, physical and spiritual.

Some people drift along without making any conscious effort to get better. They more or less surrender to life. They give up. One of the primary reasons for their attitude is the absence of any concrete goals.

Goal-setting is critical to personal growth, because goals help us focus on the things we value and help us direct our energy.

These are some of my personal goals for 1999:

- To play better basketball than I have in the first two WNBA seasons;
- To play an exciting brand of basketball that brings out the best in every athlete I play with or against;
- To help the Comets win a third consecutive WNBA championship;
- To help women's basketball grow and flourish in America and worldwide;
- To try to be a role model for inner-city youth and a person who has the best interests of youth at heart;
- To continue to do my part in the battle against breast cancer;
- To be a more loving and nurturing parent to my nieces and nephews.

What are your goals? I'd urge everyone to take the time to write down specific goals they wish to accomplish in the next year, or two years, or five years.

Going through that exercise will provide direction and focus. It will give you a blueprint for the future. Hopefully, it will light a fire within and motivate you to live your dreams.

One last word on getting better: I'd encourage every reader to devote more time to exercise and conditioning. When you're in good shape, you feel healthier and have more energy. Your self-worth and self-confidence improves, and overall you have a better attitude about life.

I know that when I'm in great shape, I'm feeling at my best. I'm more dynamic and energetic, and I feel ready and capable to take on whatever the world has to offer. That's what being in condition does for you. It's an uplifting experience. It motivates you and gets you ready for anything. It also gives you discipline, especially on days you'd rather sit on the sofa, or in a recliner, than work out.

I'm not saying you have to train like a triathlete or a marathon runner, or even be in shape to play a full-court basketball game. Just make the effort to get in good condition for your own age and body type.

Don't go overboard with a new exercise program, either; ease into it gradually. People don't get out of shape overnight, and they can't get in shape overnight. Take it step by step and slowly build up a little stamina. Take your time.

Walking, jogging, running, cycling, doing aerobics—it doesn't matter what you do, only that you do some kind of regular conditioning. Give yourself some cardiovascular exercise that elevates your heart rate and burns fat. (Just be sure to check with a physician and receive medical clearance before beginning any exercise program.)

Trust me, in the process you'll be getting better.

Chapter Twenty-six

The Courage
to Fly

So far, the second WNBA off season has proven as fast and furious as the first. I've continued working with companies like General Motors and Nike and made public appearances in Houston on behalf of the Comets.

Kim Perrot and I did an autograph session at a local mall and the manager of the Rockets Shop—which sells sportswear with the Rockets and Comets logos—reported the largest crowd ever. Fans were lined up halfway around one wing of the mall. The store manager said we pulled in more people than any Rockets player ever has. We stayed until the last autograph request was filled.

Business opportunities have continued to pop up, often from surprising places. Warner Books signed me to write this autobiographical account of my life, and Virgin Records signed me to record an R&B album, including a couple of hip-hop tracks, which the company hopes to release in 1999.

I'm excited about the album, which will provide me an opportunity to express myself and also allow me to reach a wider audience than I can playing basketball. Some people only understand a message when it's written as a song lyric or rapped in a rap song; music is the primary way they relate to communications about feelings and emotions.

I can use musical expression to help people deal with whatever problem they're having in their life. I plan to use music to express the pain, strife and uncertainty I experienced in my life and to show an empathy, and an understanding, for what people with problems are going through.

The album will be inspirational and life-affirming. We're hoping to have R. Kelly involved with the project in some capacity, because his song "I Believe I Can Fly" inspired and motivated me—as well as millions of others. R&B singer Lauryn Hill is another artist I admire greatly; I'd like the songs on my album to reflect the same kind of emotional depth as her songs.

I put my vocal chords to work shortly after the 1998 WNBA season ended. Along with Tammi Reiss of the Utah Starzz, A. C. Green of the Dallas Mavericks and Brent Barry of the Miami Heat, I narrated a series of audio books for children. The books, which feature the title character Roopster Roux, promote the value of reading. I'm sure the audio books are in stores by now.

To help me keep up with the increasing demands on my time I've hired a full-time executive assistant, Angela Wigington, who is the younger sister of my close friend Pookey Wigington. I've never been the most organized person around, but with Angela's help I'm getting better.

Angela handles my schedule and personal appearances. She also handles day-to-day operations for my new company, Coop in Motion, and new foundation, Building Dreams. One of the activities we're planning for Coop in Motion will be called Pajama Jam—a combination basketball camp and sleepover. It will combine training in basketball skills with discussions about drug use, peer pressure, teen pregnancy and resolving problems at home. We hope to conduct Pajama Jam this fall, after the 1999 WNBA season.

At the end of November, I traveled to Los Angeles to take part in a media event announcing 1999 inductees into the USC Sports Hall of Fame. I had the chance to visit with former Olympic swimmer Cynthia "Sippy" Woodhead, one of my favorite Trojans, and take in the USC–Notre Dame football game (which USC won 10–0).

Besides Sippy and me, other inductees during a black-tie dinner in May 1999 will be baseball's new home run king, Mark McGwire. I'm looking forward to meeting Mark and congratulating him on his amazing feat of 70 home runs last season. That was awesome.

It's ironic that with all my conflicts at USC—overshadowed on the court, academically ineligible and feeling like an outcast—I'm receiving such an honor. It just goes to show that anything's possible if you never give up.

This off season I've heard from USA Basketball, which has invited me to attend a training camp for U.S. Olympic team candidates in late January 1999. There's a possibility that I could compete in my third Olympiad during the 2000 Games in Sydney, Australia. Wouldn't that be something, at age thirty-seven?

Another major development during the current off season came right before Christmas. On December 22, 1998, the American Basketball League suddenly ceased operations and filed for Chapter 11 bankruptcy protection. The surprise announcement caught players and coaches alike off guard.

ABL officials said the league, which was a month into its third season, had run out of operating funds. Average attendance had fallen below 3,000 a game—well below the WNBA's average of nearly 11,000 in 1998.

The ABL's lack of a sizable television package had a lot to do with the decision. Gary Cavalli, the ABL's co-founder and CEO, said in a prepared statement, "While this was an extremely painful decision, we had no choice but to shut down. We offered millions of dollars to the TV networks for airtime but couldn't obtain adequate coverage. During the NBA lockout, the ABL still has been unable to buy TV time."

What impact the ABL's termination will have on the WNBA's third season was not immediately clear. But the WNBA overnight gained the potential to sign such former ABL standouts as Teresa Edwards, Katie Smith, Jennifer Azzi, Shalonda Enis, Clarissa Davis-Wrightsil and Natalie Williams, the league MVP in 1997–98.

If most of the top two dozen ABL players sign with the WNBA and are assigned to one of the ten existing teams or either of the two expansion teams—Minnesota and Orlando will join the WNBA in 1999—it's safe to say that our talent pool will be deeper than ever. I just hope the Houston Comets benefit from the new talent coming into our league.

When the ABL made its announcement, WNBA president Val Ackerman said, "This is an unfortunate setback for the women's sports movement. We applaud the great efforts and passion of the ABL's players and all the league and team personnel who labored so hard to start and sustain the league."

As I mentioned earlier, I've always held the view that for women's professional basketball to succeed in the United States, a league would need to draw on the financial backing and marketing savvy of the National Basketball Association.

In the end, our relationship with the NBA probably explains the difference in staying power between the two leagues. It certainly reinforces my decision to sign with the WNBA.

On one of my business trips this fall, I came across a compelling article in *Essence*, written by one of the magazine's copy editors, Sherrill Clarke. I could identify with her autobiographical story. She wrote elegantly about her shyness and timidity growing up, how she was fearful and mistrustful of others well into adulthood.

A family friend helped bring her out of her shell (much like Cristina had helped bring down my protective walls). Sherrill's friend Victor drew her out and instilled in her enough confidence to allow her to express herself. With his encouragement, she transformed herself into a bold, assertive woman.

Sherrill mustered enough self-confidence to fulfill one of her secret dreams—learning to fly an airplane. She conquered her fears and doubts.

The article, which appeared in the October 1998 issue of the magazine, was titled "The Courage to Fly." In Sherrill's case, she was speaking both literally and figuratively.

I love the image that people can fly, even soar. We have the power within us to live our dreams and make a positive impact on the world. Each of us can make a difference.

Sherrill Clarke found strength with the help of her friend Victor. I found strength with the help of my friend Cristina—and several other people, like my mom.

Now I've made a commitment to help others—not just young girls but women of all ages—find themselves and live their dreams. I am living proof that people can overcome any odds if they keep believing in themselves and don't establish any limits.

Here's my advice on developing the champion within you:

FIND YOUR GIFT

We are all unique creations of God, who endows each of us with special gifts and talents. Sometimes we don't know immediately what those talents might be, but if we keep searching, we'll ultimately find out.

Even after I found my gift—playing basketball—I felt inferior to other players, especially during my years at USC. But I didn't give up, or let my feelings of insecurity interfere with nurturing my gift. I was hungry to learn everything about basketball that I could. I took that as a challenge and didn't put any limitations on myself.

One secret for finding your gift is to be patient and wait for the Lord to show you what he has planned. Listen to your heart and allow God to work through you.

Many people grow impatient waiting for something to happen and in the process get sidetracked off the right road. It obviously takes a while for them to get back on track.

PURSUE YOUR DREAM WITH PASSION

Some people in the WNBA play basketball because they like the game or they're good at it. Some play just for money or the celebrity and fame. I play basketball because I love it.

It's my passion for basketball that drives me to work out one hour before practice, two hours during practice and another hour after practice. I don't consider that work. Practice for me is pure joy—because I love what I'm doing.

If a person is truly passionate about what he or she does for a living, it can't really be called a job, a task, a chore or work. It's fun.

When you're passionate about pursuing a dream, no sacrifice is too great. No amount of work is too much. Nothing that you go through isn't worth it. Because when you're passionate about something, you're willing to do everything in your power to succeed. You'll give your best effort every single time and you'll do so willingly.

DON'T DWELL ON THE PAST

Believe me, I was great at dwelling on the terrible aspects of my youth. I carried around a lot of baggage for many years.

Everyone is going to face unpleasant circumstances. That's part of living. It's imperative, though, to move beyond the misfortune, misery and bad occurrences because if you cling to those feelings they'll eat away at your soul.

Whatever happened, happened. It's over and done with. You can't change the past, so concentrate on what you can control—today and tomorrow. If you need to cry, cry. If you need to grieve, grieve. But then get over it. Move ahead.

There's one other relevant point here: Learn from the past. Don't keep making the same mistakes over and over. Don't keep having the same negative experiences. Learn and grow.

BE A SPONGE

This basically means learn from others. I can't begin to explain how much I learned from people like the James twins and Cristina Bertolazzi, who helped me enormously at critical junctures in my life.

Being a sponge also means soaking up information and learning new things. Don't be afraid to ask questions when you don't understand something. I used to think I was less of a person because of all the many things I didn't know; I was intimidated about asking questions because I felt by doing so I revealed my ignorance.

What keeps ignorance alive in the world is when people are afraid to ask questions, afraid to get smarter, afraid of knowledge. That's what keeps them from growing.

Being a sponge is all about growth. You're going to have different experiences in life—positive and negative ones—but personal growth and evolvement comes from learning from these experiences. Experience teaches you to see the overall picture, to make better decisions and choices, and helps you become an adult.

SURROUND YOURSELF WITH POSITIVE PEOPLE

This is one of the most crucial parts to personal growth because there's an abundance of people in this world who are negative, who will tell you what you can't do and can't accomplish. They're going to try to beat down, or extinguish, the fire that burns inside you.

There are a ton of people who will want to bring you down for a variety of reasons, including selfishness and jealousy. So it's vitally important that you surround yourself with positive people, friends who will encourage you and tell you what you can do and can accomplish.

The Lord has blessed me by putting in my life positive, upbeat people like Kim Perrot and Pookey Wigington. These are two special friends who provide everything from a pat on the back, to a shoulder to lean on or a sympathetic ear.

Pookey is the smallest (5-foot-3) giant that you'll ever meet. He's a giant in every single thing he does. He's a successful entrepreneur, and whenever he opens his mouth he has something intelligent, positive, encouraging—and important—to say. He doesn't waste words.

Kim and Pookey are the kind of friends who are unconditional with their support. They are nonjudgmental and allow me to be me. They listen to my problems and give great advice.

A. C. Green, the longtime Los Angeles Lakers star who now plays for the Dallas Mavericks, is another friend who has a positive impact on my life. When my mother's illness was getting out of hand last fall, he became a prayer partner. He also gave me advice on how to deal with this newfound celebrity and how to put everything that happens in a positive light.

I'm not used to asking for much. I'm used to shouldering burdens and responsibilities by myself. But sometimes I need to turn to others. That's when I call on Pookey or Kim or A. C. or other close friends.

Sometimes the fire inside me flickers down to the size of a tiny pilot light; it may stay that way for a night or a day or as long as a week. That's when I turn to my friends. They are so supportive and positive they'll get that flickering flame turned up again.

HANG TOUGH

I believe the Lord gives each of us only as much as we can handle. Sometimes, though, I'll say, "Can you take some of this back, Lord? My cup's a little full these days. In fact, it's running over."

Sometimes I cry all night. Sometimes I feel frazzled by all that's on my plate—from my mother's illness to my brothers and sisters making demands on me to having to address the needs of my nieces and nephews. Then there are all the demands that basketball brings.

But I hang tough because I know that being overwhelmed is part of life. Life's not simple and easy. It's neither a cakewalk nor a bed of roses. Life can be hard, even cruel.

Trust me, I speak from experience.

But if you've been knocked down, get up! If you're feeling hurt or rejected, get up! If you've been floored by emotional upheaval, get up!

The reason I say "get up!" is because only by getting up can someone move forward in life. We've all seen people get knocked down in business, or in their personal life, and never recover. They were so devastated that they gave up. Surrendered.

By hang tough, I mean stick it out when tough times occur—because they will. Hanging tough makes you a better person, adds maturity and wisdom and prepares you for the next crisis.

Hang tough means hang in there during the tough moments in your life. Don't let them get you down. If something knocks you down, get right back up. As we say in basketball—tough times don't last, tough people do.

GO THE DISTANCE

In other words, finish what you start. That includes at school, on the job, in volunteer work, playing basketball—whatever it is you're doing.

I'm not one to look back—especially now that I've learned

not to dwell on the past—but I occasionally wonder how my life would have been different if I had not returned to USC and finished my college basketball career.

Who knows, perhaps I would have become president of that bank in Inglewood. Then again, maybe not. All I know is that I would not have had the same rich experiences and dramatic personal growth if I hadn't gone the distance.

I think the terms "hang tough" and "go the distance" both apply to game two of last season's WNBA finals. We were down 12 points with seven minutes to play, and just about everyone at the Compaq Center or in the worldwide TV audience thought the Phoenix Mercury had secured the 1998 championship.

The Houston Comets, however, refused to give up. That was a difficult situation for us, but we hung tough. I always say that a basketball game lasts for 40 minutes—not 33, 38 or 39— and we were prepared to go the distance.

We could have said, "Hey, this just isn't our time. We'll try to bring it all together again next year." But life's all about finishing what you start. The Comets had started the season as favorites to defend the championship, and despite a little turmoil and a few ups and downs, we had posted a historic 27-3 record.

The whole season was on the line against Phoenix, but rather than surrender to the situation, which looked pretty bleak, we finished what we had started. The Mercury had knocked us down, but we got up. We played tough defense and came together as a team and pulled out the championship. We finished what we had started back in May. We went the distance.

Follow these seven steps and I know you will discover the champion inside you. You'll be ready to fly—even soar.

Epilogue

I'm not superstitious like some of my Houston Comets team-mates. Janeth Arcain, for example, always steps on a basketball court with her right foot first and always gets out of bed with her right leg first.

Tina Thompson is the most superstitious Comet. She has several game-day rituals, like always taking a shower after the shootaround and always putting on her uniform in a particular way. Tina must wear a red matte lipstick—Diva by MAC—every game. She has to.

I don't believe in superstitions, but I am familiar with the one about bad things happening in threes. That certainly seemed to be the case for me in the early part of December 1998.

On Monday, December 7, I had flown to Detroit to take part in my General Motors internship. No sooner had I arrived than my sister Stephanie called to say that Mother was seriously ill and had been taken to M.D. Anderson. She had been undergoing another series of chemotherapy treatments and suffered a severe reaction.

I jumped on the next plane to Houston and rushed to the hospital. When I visited with her doctors, they didn't paint a bright picture. They seemed to be saying Mother was losing the battle. Thank God, her condition gradually began to improve after several days.

On Wednesday, December 9, I stayed with her through the night. Around 4 A.M., after she woke up and we prayed together, I left to go to Kim Perrot's house. Kim was scheduled for minor surgery that day, and I had insisted on taking her to the hospital. (This minor surgery had nothing to do with the shocking news in late February 1999, when it was revealed that Kim had to undergo immediate surgery to have a tumor removed from her brain. But knowing Kim as a close friend and teammate, she's a battler and a person of great faith. I'm sure she'll recover fully.)

I had just pulled out of the Medical Center complex onto Kirby Drive and was heading over to Kim's when I was involved in a traffic accident. A teenage driver traveling in the left lane switched lanes while I was in his blind spot.

When he turned sharply to the right, the left front panel of my Mercedes collided with his back passenger door. The impact knocked the Mercedes over a curb and into a pole with a "Do Not Enter" sign. The sign referred to the drive-thru lanes of a NationsBank branch.

When my car came to rest wrapped around the pole, I was clutching the steering wheel with both hands, wondering why the air bag hadn't deployed. My door wouldn't open, so I crawled out on the passenger side and called 911 on my cellular phone.

While I was talking to a dispatcher, giving her the details of the accident and our location, a Houston policeman—Officer

Kevin M. O'Brien—arrived on the scene. He took down all the pertinent information.

A woman who had seen the other car collide with mine came running up the street and provided Officer O'Brien with a first-person account. It's not every day you can find an eye-witness at that time—4:30 A.M.—of day.

Later that morning, after my car had been towed to a local Mercedes dealership, I contacted Comets trainer Missy Leget. She immediately set up an examination with Drs. John Divine and Mark Maffet at Baylor Sports Medicine. Other than some lingering soreness in my neck and back—whiplash, I suppose—I was okay.

On Saturday, December 12, I again spent the night with my mother. I was sleeping in her room early Sunday morning when the hospital received an urgent telephone call from a paramedics unit. A nurse came to Mother's room and awak-ened me with shocking news: One of our houses in Sugar Land—the one where most of my family lives—had caught on fire.

When the fire started, my niece Brenda immediately rounded up all the children and got everyone out of the house. She tried to reach me on my cell phone, but I had turned it off so the ringing wouldn't disturb Mother.

Thank the Lord, everyone was unharmed. But the damage was substantial. What had been a two-story house was now one; the upper story had collapsed. I lost a lot of basketball me-mentos and trophies in the fire, but at a time like that you re-alize what's really important in life. And it isn't trophies and mementos.

Our neighbors were great. They came over immediately and offered to help out. The children spent the rest of the night with Ellen and Doug Earle next door.

I drove to Sugar Land as soon as I found out about the fire and let my nieces and nephews know everything would be all right. I didn't want them to be traumatized by what had happened. I spent Sunday morning on the telephone talking with insurance adjusters and then went shopping for clothes so the kids would have something to wear to school the next day.

I didn't tell my mother about the fire, at least not right away. As it was, she had enough on her mind at the hospital. But right before she was released on Monday afternoon, I filled her in on all the details. Mother was upset, naturally, but overall she took the news well. She realized the house fire could have been much worse.

My associates at General Motors and Nike were terrific. They made arrangements to send replacement Christmas gifts for the children. Raye Pond and Howard White at Nike called repeatedly to check on us. Howard, who is vice president of Brand Jordan, surprised me by arranging for several members of the Nike family of athletes—including Michael Jordan, Charles Barkley, Deion Sanders, Tiger Woods and Penny Hardaway—to call me with words of encouragement.

I also heard from Jennifer Gillom, Michelle Edwards and U.S. Olympic basketball coach Nell Fortner. And Marilyn Oshman, of the Oshman's Sporting Goods chain, came through with great support in our time of need.

I'm happy to say that our whole family had a great holiday season filled with plenty of cheer.

Around New Year's Day, I started thinking that if bad things always happen in threes, then why can't good things? That's not too much to ask for, is it? So one of the primary thoughts I'm bringing with me into the 1999 WNBA season is that the Houston Comets will win another WNBA championship. A three-peat. Three great seasons in a row.

As 1999 began, Mother's condition grew grave. The cancer she had battled so bravely and unflinchingly gained a decisive edge. By early February, her doctors informed me she was terminally ill. All that remained for them to do was monitor her medication to ease the suffering.

I started living day to day and hour to hour, doing my best to come to terms with overwhelming grief. During those long hours at the hospital, it seemed like time stood still.

Mary Cobbs passed away shortly before midnight on February 12 in Houston. That evening I had read Scripture to her, sung her favorite hymns and whispered in her ear that I loved her. I wanted Mother to hear my voice and feel my touch. I poured out my heart to her.

I had left the hospital and gone out to a late dinner when she died. I believe the Lord didn't want me to be there when he called her home. I think he knew I wouldn't have been able to handle that. I would have been too devastated.

Three nights later, at Radio City Music Hall in New York, I received another ESPY Award for Women's Pro Basketball player of the year. The ESPYs were really important to Mother and she had made me promise that, no matter what happened to her health, I would attend the event. There was no way I wouldn't be there.

I said in my brief acceptance speech that normally I accept such awards on behalf of my teammates, because basketball is a team game. But this occasion was different. "Tonight, I'd like to dedicate this award to a person who's very, very special and the most important teammate I've ever had in my entire life," I said. "And that's my mom."

I took a deep breath as applause filled my ears. "She taught me how to not be afraid to have courage, and she taught me how to use that courage to fly," I said, trying to swallow over the lump in my throat.

"So thank you, Mommy. And she's watching me from heaven."

BREAST CANCER AWARENESS

For more information on General Motors Corporation's
Concept Cure Program,
contact 1-888-GM-CCURE.

Index